Somber Waves of Grain

On Our Last Legs

By J.L. King,
A Plain American

2013 J.L. King
All Rights Reserved
ISBN-13: 978-1482635430
ISBN-10: 1482635437

I dedicate this writing to the members of my family, who for five years now have had to cope with me and my unconquerable disease called IBM, especially to my wife, Cindy, who stands by and supports me day in and day out. Without her help and the patience of all my family, neighbors and friends, this plight would be a lot worse for me.

I also dedicate this book to my fellow citizens afflicted with the grief and suffering of Myositis. I have learned from so many of you how to be strong.

May God Bless You All!

Table of Contents

Preface 7

Growing Up 9

Kennedy 24

Japan's Business Plan 26

Looking Around 35

Notions 43

Warnings 49

Under the Weather 51

Everyone's Moving On 59

Volt Shocked 62

Flashback 64

We Got School'd 70

Invasion for Political Reason 78

Conspiracy? 82

Fighting the Battle 84

Theft 89

History 95

Our Environs 98

Waking Up is hard to do 99

Stupid 104

More Stupid 106

IBM 109

Diagnosing Inclusion Body Myositis 112

Going Down 119

Show Me Your Guns 121

Gullibilitation 125

Our Money In and Out of Washington   132

Taxes   134

Paralyzed   138

Plight of the Black   140

Real MMA Fighting   142

Why did I mix my IBM & politics in this one book?   144

Epilogue   149

Preface

Unless you live in Kansas or another part of the wheat belt, you may never see the beauty of the vast fields of gluten being razzed in the southern breeze. This sight appears to be synonymous with our homeland, most going in the same direction but a few on the rebound moving in the opposite direction.

We are in the presence of a record setting drought, so those stalks of grain aren't standing as glorious as they should be at this time of their lives. If the feeble amounts of precipitation continue, there won't be a crop to harvest into our country's bread basket.

I've been blessed with a great life full of memories that could fill a semi-trailer; a very loving and creative wife, two children, now grown and married, grandchildren, nice living accommodations; and some money saved for my more golden years.

With some luck, I was able to afford college educations for my two children and paid for it all with a $10,000 investment in mutual funds years ago. After the college grads were out on their own I had enough money left in that account to purchase a ramp van, which I unfortunately require these days, but I'll get into that part of the story in a bit.

I'm worried, as farmers do every year, that the amber waves of grain are doomed to a terrible storm heading our way. As I write in this dialogue, I can see a manifestation of grief sweeping across our nation, one more dangerous that Hurricane Sandy, western wildfires, mid-western tornadoes, California earthquakes, or a drought in the breadbasket of our nation.

As I sit here at my computer, writing this manuscript, I can see the neighbor across the street installing a fence around their yard, another sign of the times. I guess I can't blame him, just to protect their two sets of twins from the outside dangers of today's world. I was raised without the fences that surround so many kids and businesses today, that in life I had the ability to make or break my day based on my decisions, not someone else's.

Chapter One

Growing Up

Growing up in north central Wisconsin offered me all kind of things when I was young...four seasons, recreation, hunting, fishing, good schools, great friends, and ample time to use them all. We didn't require a computer, Ipad or cell phone to remind us of our schedules.

I remember peddling my bike about 2 miles to the Little League field for practice, playing with a team named, "Jr. Police". Yeah, that's right.... it was sponsored by the local police department, and coached by the same. Officer Gerhke, Mr. Gerhke, or "Wally" as he had us call him, would sometimes arrive for practice in his police car, but would always change his clothes before coming onto the field to coach. We respected him not only because he was a police officer, or our coach, or a lot older and wiser that we were at the time, but because we grew up with a sense of respect for other people.

My friend, Tom B. (whose last name tortures the Polish spelling of any word with at least two "Z's") and I arrived at the field just before the scheduled time to get our team picture taken. In our haste to get our uniforms on, because we didn't make time to don our uniforms before we left home, we inadvertently switched our baseball pants. We were just pulling them up when Wally started to assemble everyone for the team photo. The Kodak camera was ready. We both bolted out of the dug out as we were attempting to fasten the top buttons of the white pants with a blue stripe running down each side. As we were running towards the home plate area, my button fastened with ease, but Tom was having great difficulty getting the button fastened, and yelled at me that we must have inadvertently switched pants in the dressing process. Tom's pants, by virtue of necessity, were several sizes larger than I needed, and I held the oversized bottom up with two hands and dashed to home plate for the photograph. Tom, on the other hand, used both hands in attempt to cover the gap of his undersized pants. The picture was taken and it showed our predicament. I still converse with Tom on Facebook, and often laugh at that day at Boileau Field. I hope to run across that picture someday and share it on FB with all our friends.

Before moving from Wisconsin, my son and I visited the local library where we were able to search the local newspaper archives and rekindle my memories of those 'good ole days' when the local paper took time to write articles and print box scores from all the areas Little League game action. Both Tom's name and my name were often found in the article for pitching or hitting success. I was a catcher, so I didn't get too much press on the mound.

Tom and I also attended high school together. Our Catholic education, a great extra expense to our parents, provided us with the chance to lead the songs during mass for our entire student population. I think we did that for two or three years, before graduating with the Class of '69". I haven't seen him much since graduation, so today's Facebook popularity is a Godsend. I purchased a Vox Country-Western guitar in 1967 (when Country-Western music wasn't cool), and still have it today. It's still in like new condition, although it had a lot of playing time on it. I just wish I could still use it.

I had another close friend who lived about three blocks from me. He was a year older, but we enjoyed our Scouting years together, and later our high school years. Since he was a year older than me, Mike had his driver's license sooner. He picked me up every morning in his mother's Plymouth, yes, the model that had a push button shift control on the left side of the dash panel rather than a shift lever. I think it was a 1963 or 1964 Plymouth Belvedere, sort of a taupe color. I'm sure he would have had it painted a different color if it were his car. Mike's dad was a naval pilot and I could spend hours admiring the aircraft photos that he had framed in their rec room. After college, Mike married his high school sweetheart, but their lives were shattered in a hunting death of their oldest son. I've tried to make contact with him, but really haven't heard or seen him since the early 70's, but I did learn that he and his high school mate had parted the sheets years ago.

My best friend going through grade school and high school was named Rich. He lived on the south side of town, but every other week our parochial school "Bluebird" bus would take us north siders to the south side to pick up the kids living there. The opposite weeks, Rich would get to ride to the north side of town when our side got picked up first in the morning and dropped off first after school. Rich moved to California when we were juniors in high school, a day that really saddened me. Rich went on to be a successful physician, and still resides in California.

My childhood grew around the fact that we were only middleclass at best, with my father working as a truck driver for Nabisco, and my mother as a school teacher, first for a small catholic school, then onto the public school system. Not a lot of money in those days, but enough to always make us kids happy.

Although we never had some of the exotic vacations as some of our friends encountered, we always had food on the table, never lacked for an after-school snack and usually took time out for an annual vacation. My favorite vacation spot was in Door County, Wisconsin, in Egg harbor, in a historic home with a Cupola. The Cupola House, built in 1871, was placed on the National Registry of Historic Sites in July of 1979. The house was built by Levi Thorpe who paid for the building of his house from gold dust he had brought home from the California gold rush. I remember my Dad telling me that he was so selective in what lumber could be used in its construction that no lumber with knots were allowed to be used. The floors were made from some of the clearest white pine material from Wisconsin's ample forest offerings that I have ever seen. My dad rented the first floor of that Cupola House from Rocky Fairchild, a salesman for Nabisco at that time, and upon occasion when the owners were there we got to climb up the winding staircases to the cupola on top of the world and see the vast expanse of Lake Michigan as the wives and mothers of now ancient mariners did a century ago.

Decades later, I returned to Egg Harbor with my wife, Cindy and two children of our own, and the old Cupola House is still there, probably still as strong as the day it was built, but now has been converted into a gift shop. All of the out buildings that used to be on the property have since been torn down, and the once large lot surrounding the Cupola House, now contains a paved drive and parking lot for gift shop patrons, and some permanent park-like picnic tables were added to accommodate tourists stopping in for a break. As I stepped into the gift shop, I recalled my sister yelling and screaming at me for putting a dead alewife fish down the back of her swimsuit when at the local beach. Not nice, but isn't that what brothers are for? I still often visit this area on the Google Earth website as a tool to remember this King vacation mecca.

I don't think it was placed on the National Historic Registry because we stayed there, but it's neat to be able to say we vacationed in that grand place several times during our younger years. I still have a framed picture of the Cupola House hanging in my house today.

Cupola House
Egg Harbor, Wisconsin

My father left Nabisco when they decided to consolidate the warehouse operation in a different city. He found a loan to purchase a seafood distributorship in our home town of Wausau, Wisconsin. Goodbye cookies, hello seafood. Lloyd's Seafoods, as it was named, distributed all kinds of frozen seafood to area restaurants. As Wisconsin is known for its "Friday Fish Fry", there were plenty of prospective clients to sell to. He would travel to Green Bay each Monday to pick up frozen product that he had called in on the previous Friday, and made a number of stops on his trip back to Wausau. He had an established route each day of the week. His clients, depending on their restaurants, might require anywhere from 8 pounds of frozen haddock, cod or Pollock, to supply Friday night fish fry patrons, to larger customers who in their small establishments would take 200 pounds of fish, shrimp, scallops, and lobster and cases of French fries in straight or crinkle cut each week. Once a month, he would travel about 20 minutes east of the City of Green Bay and purchase some of the best "smoked chubs" that I have ever tasted. I remember visiting that smoke shop one time while accompanying my Dad on his Monday trip. We got to sample some warm, freshly smoked fish that had just come out of the smoker. It didn't get much better than that!

There was one particular stop in the middle of nowhere, along old Highway 29, that was known for its good fish frys. On any given Friday night, you could spend a longer time waiting at the bar for a table, than it took to be seated, order your food, get served and complete your meal. The proprietor, Roger Breske, (same name as my mother's maiden name, but no relation) was a walking people encyclopedia. He knew everyone by name, knew what they normally drank, and asked about your family, regardless of how long it was since your last visit. He worked at a frantic NASCAR pace behind the bar. On any given Friday night, people would be stacked three deep around the large oval shaped bar, and Roger could keep a conversation going with all of them.

On the other hand, Lloyd's Seafood had some other customers that adorned the opposite side of the customer service spectrum. I remember one in particular whose largest order was probably only two 4-pound boxes of the least expensive fish that Dad sold, and he complained about the price if it went up only a couple cents a pound or even if it didn't go up in price. We did patronize him for a fish fry one Friday, and learned that his demeanor was the same with his clientele, thus the lack of business for him.

I always looked forward to Fridays, as we often went out for one of those fish fries. We were raised Catholic, and at that time, no-meat on Fridays was the norm. I often wondered how not eating meat on Fridays was a sacrifice when I enjoyed and looked forward to going out for a fish fry.....sort of contradicted the whole sacrifice thing.

As I periodically would take over my Dad's route when Mom & Dad would need to get away for a vacation or meeting, I got to meet all of the customers and experience the differences between them. But above all, I always treated them respectfully, whether a large customer or small.

I was fortunate, very fortunate....that my father was raised on a farm about six miles away. It was there that I learned an appreciation for machinery, something that I would later in life turn into my career. After grade school was out for the year, I practically lived on that family farm for the summer. I barely remember my Grandfather, Henry, and my Grandmother. Helen is only remembered from my early years. My uncle Ervin now owned the farm after Grandpa died and Grandma moved to town, then later passed. Uncle Erv never married. He was too busy, I guess. His farm's equipment was his children. I mean that. He bought brand new IH tractors every couple of years. He taught me the necessity to keep up on the cleaning and maintenance of equipment, because at trade in or selling time, he would always get top dollar for his used gear. He would often receive phone calls on the rotary dial phone that sat on the desk in the dining room of the old farmhouse, asking him when he would be ready to sell one of his tractors or combines, because they wanted to buy it, and were willing to pay top shelf prices.

My memory recollects being on the farm the day when he took delivery of a new tractor. The delivery guy wanted to show him how to drive it and suggested they take a ride down the ¼ mile long gravel driveway. My uncle told the delivery guy, that the tractor wasn't going to take any ride down the dusty driveway until it had a coat of his favorite and special wax applied. I think it was call Astro-Shield, probably a "wax of the future" that probably wouldn't compare to the car waxes of today. But it worked for him. We were standing near this new tractor after the wax had been applied and witnessed a small bird trying to land on top edge of the tractor's hood. The bird was too close to the edge and couldn't keep his footing on the slippery, waxed finish. My uncle's equipment always looked good, and my cousins and I were proud to be able to operate and maintain them as such.

I often stayed on Uncle Erv's farm for weeks on end during the summer break from school, but he always insisted that I peddle my ass to every baseball practice and game, "never miss one", he would say. I didn't have to get up at 5:00 AM to help with cow milking, but all the equipment needs for the day better be fueled, greased and ready to go when he was ready to hit the fields. He paid me well and I had great times "at work" with cousins Tom & Jim. Being paid well during my early years of ages 9 thru 13 was something that most other kids were never able to appreciate. Never being able to find time to spend the money was something, that at the time, I didn't appreciate, but now as an adult I do.

During the school year when I was at home, I was given to tools to make more money. My father and Uncle Irv had made a homemade garden tractor, about 6' long and 3' wide. They took the rear axle from a Chevy they found at the local junkyard, and craftily cut down the housing and axle shaft to make the appropriate width. I forget what the 3-speed transmission was from, but I remember the Briggs and Stratton engine, with a crank start on it, not fun starting on sub-zero days, but I learned a knack of how to do it and could often start the engine even when my dad could not get it started. They built homemade implements for that tractor also...snowplow, a single bottom plow, cultivator, potato planter, leveling drag, etc., everything but a mower attachment. I had a motorized push mower to do that job. There wasn't much around the yard that wasn't easily handled by that tractor and attachments. We had a large garden that connected to the gardens of two neighbors to the north of us, so there was a lot of plowing that took place every year. The combined garden was approximately 300 feet long by 75 feet wide that was actually part of the railroad right of way that ran in back of our homes. When spring plowing season came, that little tractor saw lots of work, then the potato planting attachment was busy, along with the cultivator to keep the weeds in check and the soil aerated.

That garden produced mass quantities of beets, lettuce, peas, sweet corn, potatoes, radishes, cucumbers, watermelons, squash, and other vegetables for the table and canning jars. We also had rhubarb plants where I would often sit with a cup of sugar and eat right from the patch of the fast growing rhubarb. When my mother noticed she was missing some coffee cups from the cupboard, she would summon me to go out to the rhubarb patch and bring some back in the house.

I remember during one of my mom's canning sessions, she sent me downstairs to fetch some empty canning jars from the shelf in the corner of the basement. Low and behold, a friendly skunk had nosed a little too far into one of the basement window screens and fell into our basement. As you can imagine, this was not a good situation. One of my parents called the police department to ask if they knew of a safe way to get the skunk out of the basement, but they declined to have any knowledge in that predicament. Luckily, someone heard of our problem and suggested that we put a wooden plank from the basement floor up through the same window that it had fallen through, and the skunk would probably find its own way out, as it didn't want to be stuck in our basement any more than we wanted him to be there. It was also suggested that we place pieces of sardines to lure the skunk, now probably very hungry, along the plank and sprinkle the plank with some flour so we could see the tracks indicating that it had "walked the plank" and was out of the lower level of our home. We were also told it would be a way to see, to the opposite of our plan, if more skunks or varmints entered our basement in the meantime. To our elation, there was a single track path heading up the plank and to the outside when we checked in the morning. A heavier duty basement window screen was installed and canning season continued.

When I was about 10, I took over as the chief operator of that little homemade garden tractor. A few people in our suburban neighborhood called and asked if they could hire me to plow their gardens for them. Of course, I accepted. Plowing one garden usually turned into a second, then a third, and on and on. I started plowing gardens in a three block radius from our house, but soon ventured out to as far as a mile from our house.

Gas was only about 30 cents a gallon then, and I rarely used more than a quarter tank for most people's small gardens. Luckily there was a gas station only two doors from our house, so the walk with the five gallon can being pulled in a wagon wasn't too difficult. Elmer, the gas station owner, saw me as an honest young man, and allowed me to fill up my gas can by myself, and leave the money on his cash register so he wouldn't have to leave the repair job he was working on. At a later time, he paid me as an attendant to take care of the gas filling for customers. In those days, the attendant not only filled up the customer's gas tanks, but also washed windows, checked the engine oil level, checked the alternator belt tension and sometimes checked and filled the air pressure in the auto's tires if the customer requested it.

I usually charged between $5 & $8 to plow small or medium sized gardens and customers happily paid it to get the job done. For large gardens, clients would happily pay $10. Their alternative method of spending hours of turning the soil over by hand with a garden spade was reason enough to pay the price. Often they offered me more or gave me a couple of dollars as a tip, and usually provided me with a work break filled with Kool-Aid or milk and cookies.

After a couple of years, I had some competition to work against. A guy down the street had built a knock-off copy of my homemade tractor, and tried to weasel his way into my business. But the unreliable, cocky service experiences that he often exhibited drove the customers back to me, and in greater numbers. More and more people in our suburban neighborhood started gardens on their spare plots of land, and I benefited from almost all of them. I had to carry my Little League baseball game schedule with me at all times so I could make and meet my appointments with my customers. No cell phone, no Ipad, no anything electronic to use as a reminder, but I never missed an appointment for doing a garden job. Imagine that.

In the winter time, I would mount the snowplow on the front of the tractor and plow snow for people in our neighborhood. There were some doctors and dentists that lived along the Wisconsin River on the other side of the train tracks that skirted the lot line at the rear of our house and they were prime candidates for needing their driveways cleaned. They weren't the best clients because you really had to chase them to get paid, or they didn't have any small bills, so they said. So, at 5:00 AM on school days after a night of Wisconsin snow, I would get dressed in the warmest closes I had, go out to the garage, do some shoveling so I could get Mom's car out of the garage to access the emergence of the world's best snowplow machine. I usually did our 85′ long driveway and four other driveways before I would have to go home, eat a bit of breakfast and catch the 7:30 arrival of our school bus. Usually, I would have to repeat that procedure after school, and it was always a good time to knock on the door of customers to get paid.

I learned an interesting thing about collecting money from my clients. I learned that rather than charging them a set amount based on how much snow we received, or by whom I was doing the work for, I would simply say, "Give me what its worth to you". In every case, I received more money than I probably would have charged for the job. This worked with all types of clients; doctors, dentists, retirees, old widows or young married couples. I continued that approach during the following winters and carried it over to my spring garden plowing jobs.

I had one doctor who hadn't paid for the last two driveway plowings, and we got an enormous snowstorm that dumped about 12 inches of snow on everyone in the neighborhood. Since he didn't pay for the last two, I didn't plow his driveway in the early morning, and he had to call a commercial snow plowing service that charged him a little more than twice what he owed me. That evening he came over to the house, paid me in full plus money for the next snowstorm, so he could get back on my before-school list of customers.

I became successful as a young garden-plowing, snow clearing entrepreneur that there were weeks when I brought home more money than my Dad made putting in his 40 hour weeks with Nabisco. When I learned how much of a Dad pride-buster that was, I started keeping the profit report to myself.

I wish cameras where more available in those days, as I do not have any pictures of that old tractor. But the memories of using it and the memories of all that I gained from that homemade tractor still remain with me today. My only regret is that all the money I made as a kid had no state or federal taxes paid from it.....yeah, right!

When I was 14, I spent some of that money.......paid for an outing to the Philmont Scout Ranch in New Mexico with my friend, Rich, and a Canadian canoe trip with my local Scout Troop 411. What a summer we had. A long train ride to Colorado Springs, Colorado, followed by a long bus hike to the scout ranch in New Mexico, two weeks home, then a 3-vehicle caravan from central Wisconsin to the boundary waters on the Minnesota/Canada border. Different than a lot of other kids who rode those trips on the coattails of their parent's wallets, I earned every last penny for those trips. It was a lot of work, sometimes, hot hard work, but rewarding. I wouldn't trade those days for anything!

Scouting was a huge benefit in my life. I always had great leaders, who put in an enormous amount of time supporting us. A lot of things that I do every day now come at the pleasure of learning it while in the Scouts. People often ask where I learned to do certain things, and the answer is usually the same...hone, farm or Scouts. We learned and practiced respect, again something that is also going the way of the Do-Do bird today. I earned my cooking merit badge on a hiking campout. I borrowed one of my mother's bread baking pans and placed a frozen loaf of bread dough in it and placed it under the top flap of my backpack. When we arrived at the campgrounds after the long hike, I removed the pan from my backpack and placed it in a rock oven that I constructed next to the fire. About 45 minutes later, I sliced a couple pieces of warm baked bread, placed it on a plate with some butter slathered on top and presented it to our scoutmaster. Along with the other requirements for this merit badge, his signature indicating I earned that award came pretty easy.

Mom's mother, passed away shortly after Mom was born, so I never met her, and did not we hear much about her. Leo, my Grandpa, worked at the Brokaw Paper Mill, (later known as Wausau Papers), but retired during my younger years. I remember him coming to visit us almost every day, and we always looked forward to the candy bar he would have stashed in his pocket for us kids. Grandpa was the influence that I had to later enjoy hunting and fishing. He would often pick me up in his 1952 Chevy, or later in his 1959 Chevy Biscayne to go fishing on one of Wisconsin's trout fishing streams or lakes. We would usually come home with a nice catch, that we would methodically clean and place in the freezer for later consumption. We would always dig a hole in the garden to bury the fish "guts", something that I learned was a good form of fertilizer for the abundant produce we grew there.

I remember the time when Grandpa was shopping for a new car. Before sealing the deal on any auto purchase, he would ask the car sales man to open the trunk of the new car so he could physically evaluate where his favorite fishing pole would fit in the trunk. If it didn't fit, no deal.

Grandpa Leo would take me fishing and hunting a lot, when I was not working on the farm. When I was real young, he started me out with some target shooting in a lonely part of an area called Nine Mile Swamp. Nine Mile Swamp was a desolate area in Marathon County of vast forest and swamps about 15 miles from our house, and the stories I heard was that if you got lost in it, you probably wouldn't be able to find your way out. Today, that area contains many snowmobile and ATV trails, and I doubt if anyone could get lost there even if they tried. My firearm training progressed from killing "tin cans" to squirrel and rabbit hunting, then onto grouse (he called them Partridge), then deer hunting. My father was also a deer hunter, so I was always a hunting companion for one or even both of them.

My first deer kill was a long shot in another swampy area 25 miles east of Wausau. It was on a place known as "Paradise Island", that I shot a 206 pound buck on the second day of the season when I was 14 years old. We had our rope to pull him with, and it took two of us at all times pulling on the rope across a snowless ground surface. This heavy, six pointer with a busted up set of antlers was shot about 2 miles from the car, so we had to drag it off the "island", surrounded by a swamp, through the woods to a field area where Dad could drive his car to. Because of the lack of snow and the long distance that we dragged this deer, most of the hair on one side of the buck's fur was rubbed off by the rough ground conditions. The deer hardly fit into my Dad's Candy Apple Red '66 Ford Mustang. When transporting a deer in those days, you could put the deer in the trunk, but a leg with the Department of Natural Resources tag had to be showing. It wasn't much problem to let the tag show, because most of the deer was outside the trunk area during the trip home. I didn't mind the small trunk, after all, it was my first deer kill, and I was proud of it.

In my younger years, we played a lot of cops & robbers, cowboys & Indians, good guys & bad guys. We begged our mothers to purchase ammunition for our cap guns at age 6. We had cap guns that looked like western handguns and some that looked like western rifles. We often pointed them at cars driving past our house and no one every complained about it. Not one of us ended up being a career thief or mass murderer.

My younger sister often reminds me of the time when we were playing cowboys and Indians and I tied her up to a tree a bit away from home. About 15 minutes later, my parents tried to gather us up so we could get ready to attend a wedding ceremony and wondered where my sister was. Whoops, guess I forgot something outside and rushed to the spot where she was still tied up, released her and hurried her home to get ready for the wedding. Nowadays, I would have been demonized as being politically incorrect playing "Indians", unlawful possession of a toy that looked like a real firearm, kidnapping, and/or illegal detention of another person. My rap sheet (at the age of 9) would have been posted in every government computer, post office, and watch list, and my name would probably be readily available on someone's neighborhood watch list. How things have changed.

Chapter Two

Kennedy

We had air raid drills in school at least once a month. The civil defense warning system put in place in case of an attack on our country was practiced regularly in those days. During a drill that only took a couple of minutes, we had to crouch down under our desks, and roll up into a little ball. As I think about it now, I'm not sure what good that actually would have done if a nuclear event would have happened. It was years later that I learned of the reason why we needed them and how close we were to needing them in real life. With the USA being played by the Communists in Russia their actions were delayed by reactions President Kennedy took a risk on. I should use the word "delayed", because they were never totally defeated. I now know they were actually here to stay and remain here today, perhaps not in the form we all envisioned, with the necessary bomb shelters and civil defense preparations, but they are still here working every day to take us over. And realizing what is taking place these days their long term planning abilities are taking a toll on America today.

I remember that day in November, 1963. Kennedy was assassinated when I was in the 7th grade at St. James Catholic School. When the principal came in and told us what had happened, a troublemaker in the class stood up and pretended to be shooting with a pair of handguns. Not good, not appropriate. I knew that family members would be sad over the event as we often heard them sing his praise, and knew everyone in our relation probably voted for him. I remember going to see the movie, PT109 with a neighborhood friend. I remember everyone talking about the Communists, and how they could spoil that something special that we have here in America.

During the elections in the following years, there was usually someone running that represented the Communist Party that tried to obtain some voting interest. No one ever believed that a professed member of the Communist party would ever exceed in being elected to the highest office in the land. And I guess they were right. No President has ever been elected out of the Communist Party to date, or at least by that party name.

Kennedy is the Democrat that everyone always remembers. When seniors say they are a Democrat, they will usually refer back to JFK, and probably wouldn't vote for any other party because of him. And I have no problem with that, unless their remembrance of him is the only reason for voting that way. Things change, parties change, voters need to stay current also.

Today, we really don't know what we are voting for. The party names are the same, but their ideologies have changed. We will talk about that later.

Chapter Three

Japan's Business Plan

Because of my college major attempt at becoming an Audiologist came to an end in 1972, I took a job at the company that two of my other uncles worked at. I started on the crane assembly line putting together crane booms. A year later, I took a post sub-assembling the engine modules for the same crane line, but it was on the day shift. Business was good, and we usually worked 10 or twelve hours a day and at least five hours on Saturday and even some Sunday work was offered toward the end of each month when product had to be completed for shipment. I didn't have too much time to spend my money, and sometimes found my wallet filled with four or five un-cashed checks, before I made a trip to the bank. In 1975, I accepted a job at the company's R & D Center, using my audiology experience from my college attempt to get a job in the Sound and Vibration Lab.
My work partner Jim B. made a great team working together in that lab, and our passions for snowmobiles and snowmobile racing threaded a common bond between us. We worked together for about two years until I heard of a job opening in the Travelift Installation Group.

My title was Travelift Erection Supervisor. I got to travel to various corners and midsections of many countries and assembled a team of local workers and erected these large mobile gantry type cranes usually used in the pre-stress concrete industry. This is the job that started my international travels. In 1978, I traveled down to Venezuela five times during the year to erect eight Travelifts in various parts of their country. It was during this timeframe that I met my soon-to-be wife, and being gone on the road after meeting this terrific woman was pure torture. Travelifts were erected in record times just so I could get home to see her. My soon Bride-to-be, did inflict an uncomfortable experience on me when she printed in the local newspaper that I was employed as an "Erection Supervisor" for our company. Needless to say, I took an extreme amount of kidding the next few weeks in the manufacturing plant and offices. Cindy, my new wife & I spent 6 weeks together in the Tacoma, Washington area starting a few days after returning home from our honeymoon in Miami Beach, Florida in 1979. In 1980, I had enough of that road job and took a position as Reliability Supervisor for our Service and Sales Group.

In 1981, after I had 9 years of Construction Equipment industry experience under my belt, our Sales and Service Group was gathered up in our north central Wisconsin office and was told that our parent company was moving and consolidating all Product Sales and Service personnel to their corporate headquarters in Racine, WI. It was a pretty sad day considering that two weeks prior to that announcement, we received a letter from a corporate vice-president telling us that a consolidation was just a rumor and in no way should be taken seriously by anyone. For the short time between those events, everyone was happy.

The announcement of the consolidation came as a surprise after returning from the Christmas and New Year holidays. It was especially troubling for my wife and me, as we were expecting our first child in May. Our direction from corporate was that we had to report to their offices in about four weeks, and immediately plan on selling our homes and get ready to move. It was almost the end of February when we actually did report to our new office location, and even longer than that to receive our relocation packages that explained our direction in selling our homes by ourselves or enter into an agreement with the company for a relocation purchase plan. Everyone wondered what we were getting ourselves into when it was evident that the move was announced before all the irons in the fire were identified and resolved.

During our first couple of months in the new makeshift office in southeastern Wisconsin, none of the dozen or so people who were instructed to report there had an assigned office desk. We had to find out who was traveling or on vacation and not going to be in the office on a given day, and get there early enough to grab that desk to use for the day. We also found out that we would have to interview to keep our current jobs.

The timing couldn't have been worse. It is now mid-March. Our first child is due in a couple of months. A two hundred-twenty mile trip to do any house hunting was denied by my wife's doctor. I had to explain this to the powers to be at our corporate office. I did, and they wouldn't accept it. I had to be there every day if I wanted to keep my job. My request was denied to delay my move until after the baby had arrived. All of a sudden, it looked like I wouldn't have a job in a bad economy right before the arrival of a new family member.

Fortunately for me, all, and I mean all of the other group members staged a meeting with that supervisor and talked him into keeping me on the team. It worked because I was allowed to keep my job and did not have to move until after the birth of our daughter, Laura Ann.

It was a tough point in our lives. In a 1.5 month timeframe, we had welcomed our new offspring into the world, had her baptized and had the party that goes along with it, shopped and bought a house in a distant land (230 miles away) at a whopping 15.25% home loan interest rate, sold our home through a company relocation plan, started a new job in a new city, physically moved our household, and...I spent five days in Port-au-Prince, Haiti....all in less than a two month period. Talk about packing a lot of life "events" into a short period of time.

Cindy didn't like driving in large city traffic, and I can still see her from my review mirror, crushing the steering wheel with her bare hands while driving almost up on the bumper of my pickup truck. I had the new born baby girl with me in a car seat on the seat next to me, and fortunately she decided to sleep through Milwaukee's traffic. It was an uneventful trip for baby Laura and me, but my wife's nerves were shot by the time we reached our destination.

What I learned during the next six months in corporate office life was that the company was very big on 5-year planning, but very short in executing that plan. Most of the commitments that were made out of the five year plan lasted only about six months, then it was back to the old direction or some new VP would cancel the current plan in favor of doing something new and exciting to him that had already been tried before his arrival and was already proven a failure. Ditto, ditto.....more of the same for several years.

There were many years of losing millions of dollars each year, but we had a sugar daddy named Tenneco. Vice presidents were changed more often than underwear. At one point in time, our corporate office had more than 35 Vice Presidents ..... at one time! Someone wore a T-shirt to a company picnic one year that said, "If you aren't VP, you aren't shit!" No wonder a plan was ever allowed to be carried out. Some new VP always had a better idea. We had new VP's from almost every walk of life. From the aerospace industry to diaper manufacturers, we got them all, all claiming to be the next savior of our farm and construction equipment company. All short timers, too. I remember going to a meeting with our group where a new VP was to be introduced. The new VP was introduced to us, and he spent the next 15 minutes telling us about all the various companies and positions he has held in the past. An old veteran employee sitting next to me leaned over and quietly said to me, "It sounds like this guy can't hold a job!" How right he was because the new VP moved on about a year later.

During the second year at the corporate location, a presentation called, "The Japanese Challenge" was offered to members of our sales and service group. This was one of the best presentations that I can remember. The presentation encompassed the automotive plan of the Japanese automakers to take over the car industry in the USA. Their plan started in the late 60's, with a resulting milestone accomplishment in the 90's. Wait a minute. We couldn't grasp onto a business plan for more than 6 months at a time and the Japanese are in the fifteenth year of their thirty year plan? Impossible? True? We now know the answer to that short question.

The Japanese plan was to enter the US market slowly in the early 70's, which they did. Their products were inferior at the time and most of us remember seeing some of those cars with rust up to the door handles, and ropes holding the trunks closed. On the first cold day approaching winter, one could hardly count the number of "foreign" cars found dead along our country's highways.   Japanese businessmen conceded large auto sales for the first 10 years, but used the naïve American consumer as proving grounds for their products. These same businessmen concluded that their cars would not sell well in the USA as long as the principle buyers were pre-World War II born. For sure, no veteran of WWII or anyone close to a vet of that war would settle for a Japanese automobile. After all, our association with Japan was so stressed that we had to drop two atom bombs to end the discussion with them in the 40's. People remember things like that.

If the Japanese automakers could develop their cars for the USA market by the mid 1980's, they would have a shot at being a major player by the 90's. Yup, when the WWII soldiers started to hit the rocking chairs in retirement, the Toyotas, Nissans & Hondas of the world would have developed and proven cars for their target market, ready to sell to us baby boomers and all that follow.

And so, there lies the story of the Japanese auto market in the USA. Not a six month plan, not a five year plan, but a robust 30 year plan. Were they successful? I'd say so. It is evident that their initial plan also included building automotive manufacturing plants here in the USA to locally make their products. They saw that labor unions were hurting the industry, so they envisioned their successes based on non-union involvement. For the most part, they have become very successful with that notion.

By the mid 90's, the Japanese automakers had successfully implemented and carried out their plan, to the tune of "We are Number 1"!

In comparison, many American businesses are still working with their 6 month and 5 year business plans only to be trounced on by better business planning on foreign soils.

Shortly after moving to Wichita, KS in 1995, I read an article on how the Japanese company, Honda, was planning to enter the small business jet industry within the next 20 years. Wichita is a hub for manufacturing small business jets. Cessna, Learjet, Hawker Beechcraft, and hundreds of supporting vendors call Wichita their home. Boeing was also located here, but sold their Wichita operations out to Spirit Aerospace, who still continues to build fuselages for Boeing passenger jets here in this city. The news of the Honda plan to enter the business jet market shook a few tails here in Wichita. For years, there seemed to be no press regarding Honda's progress in this market, but in recent years, photographs and articles are becoming more ostensible, proving more long term planning by the Japanese. Japan was quietly planning, and is still quietly planning a makeover and takeover of American ingenuity with some of their own.

Other counties, namely China used their long range business plan to solidify their identity. China's long range planning capability plan advanced their movement by supporting the globalization of product manufacturing. Their target was much larger than the Japanese plan, and encompassed more coverage in the world. They wanted to be the world's center for manufacturing. I think they are being successful. But China's long term business plan was more one-sided than others. They wanted world globalization but strongly desired the manufacturing to be in their country. For a couple of decades, their government furnished incentive money to offset costs of building new manufacturing plants there and being able to lure USA business to a cheaper method of manufacturing their goods across the pond rather than on USA soil. American businesses bit on that hook, line and sinker, and off to China our manufacturing jobs went. That was great for American company's profits, but bad for American jobs. Once moved to China, it was hard financially justifying the return of that manufacturing to our country.

The Chinese have also made great strides to purchase as many textile factories close to the USA in Mexico. Once they dominate that market, they will be able to raise clothing prices to make huge profits.

Along with the transfer of our manufacturing went a lot of manufacturing expertise and usually tooling to make various products. Giving the Chinese the ability to see and dissect our American manufactured machine tools, allowed them to quickly copy, improve and mass produce similar tooling for their own use. Business leaders and our government today are screaming about how the Chinese have been stealing our technology. It's pretty easy when we mass-ship our tooling to American soil for them to emulate. What about the Chinese computer hackers who have been successful in getting into government and corporate files and computer systems? Didn't we make that task easier by allowing such open communications via our computers to theirs?

On a trip to China in 2004, I had the opportunity to visit a Chinese manufacturer's assembly plant in a city about 3 hour's drive south of Shanghai. I contently watched the speedometer of the new Buick minivan that was transporting us. The speedometer constantly was seen as reading 125 to

130 kph, which translates to about 80 mph. For most of that 3 hour drive, I also noticed a constant stream of fairly new manufacturing plants…..on both sides of the road. Now, I didn't count them, nor would I have been capable of counting them, but I bet I saw over 5000 factories during that 3 hour drive at 80 mph, lined up on both sides of this beautiful and ultra-smooth six lane divided highway. The remarkable fact is that the 5000 guesstimate is just the ones lined up on highway facing property. How many more where stacked up off the highway and out of sight? How many thousands more brand new factories were located in their country's cities and other provinces?

During that trip, I felt I saw the insides of every Wal-Mart, K-Mart & Target stores line up along the highway. Yes, brand after brand of names that we purchase on a regular basis, many of which I didn't even realize had factories in other parts of the world, were all proudly assembled for me to see along this highway.

USA road construction engineers ought to take a trip to see some of the Chinese highways. Hit by similar winter freezing temperatures that we realize here in the states, most of their road construction outlasts the expensive roads paid for by our tax dollars. The four-year old road on which I traveled 3 hours (actually six hours, with the return trip), were magnificently smooth, and void of the potholes we so admire here in our country. Hell, you couldn't even feel the seams between the highway and bridge crossings.

Maybe it was the speed at which we were traveling or cruising for such a long ride, but I was immensely impressed with many of their roads…while our government would like you to only envision the 100 year old Chinese cart path roads of yesteryear.

I think that the globalization effort in America was part of someone's 30 year master plan to defeat America, not strengthen it or the world. Am I the only one who when hearing the term "globalization" immediately thought of lost jobs? Am I the only one in this country that saw the effects of lost jobs when the North American Free Trade Agreement (NAFTA) agreement was signed with Mexico? I hope not.

Chapter Four

Looking Around

In 1986, five whole years since the birth of our first child, Cindy and I were blessed with a second one. As I am 6'2" and my wife is 5'12" (she thinks it sounds shorter than 6' for a woman), neither of our babies was small. This boy was no different. Twenty-four inches at birth was just a start of a man named David that grew to 7' tall. Yes, seven feet, eighty four inches, 2.13 meters, 2133 millimeters……. There weren't enough cows in Wisconsin to satisfy this boy's thirst for milk. Yes, he played basketball, which was most in part of how I put two kids through college on $10,000 with some help of a couple of good mutual funds. But David's favorite sport in life was baseball.

Being six foot, ten inches and throwing from a raised mound on a Maize KS High School just wasn't fair to any batter. He accomplished 18 wins and zero losses during his high school career, not many by most standards, but if you consider the game limitations placed on high school teams in Kansas, each team was only allowed 20 games a year, and since there were several pitchers, all had to be extended their opportunity to pitch. David helped two of his high school teams to state tournament titles. David seldom talks about his previous coaches, except for one, Rocky Helm, his high school varsity baseball coach.

Laura, on the other hand, involved herself with several school clubs, and even spent a year as a flag "twirler" with the high school marching band. I remember attending a couple marching band competitions, one at Kansas University Memorial Stadium, and again at Kansas State University Family Stadium. A few years later, Laura enrolled at Kansas University in Lawrence, KS, and had the privilege of working with the famed KU basketball team as one of the trainer assistants, then as a team ambassador.

Planning ahead for both myself and our now family of four, I recognized that I must provide a better future for them. In 1990, I put in for a job at corporate for a position as Product Support Manager for our company's International Business Unit (IBG). My resume was either complete enough to get me that job, or everyone else was afraid of it. The territory that I was responsible for was not small. The new territory was the whole globe, with the exception of the USA, Canada and Western European Countries. Not bad though for a guy that started tinkering with a homemade garden tractor.

We had saved up a little money besides what we had invested in some mutual funds to help defray the college tuition costs in the years to come. Although that came at the expense of not living anywhere near a lavish lifestyle, we always scraped up enough money to afford several camping trips a year with a great family that we became associated with at work. Martin was a Brit, from Argentina, and his wife, Margarita was Colombian. Their daughter, Jackie, born here, rounded out their family. All three were a learning experience that we really enjoyed and I hope they felt the same about us. Martin and Margarita took the path of becoming naturalized citizens, and Jackie was born here as a certified USA citizen. Crazy times we will always remember.

From my position in the IBG, I got to see a lot of interesting places in the world, not from the perspective of a tourist, but by working with people with dirt and grime on their hands. Working with the people is a lot different from seeing the lands from a tourist perspective. As a tourist, you are looking to be made happy, whereas as a support manager, you were counted on by the company and the customers to make the customers happy, a big difference. I know friends and relatives who have dabbled in some overseas travel, and have come up with some very different analysis of other countries as tourists compared to my working man's perspective. Tourists see the bright, rosy side of almost everything. If you don't take time to dive into what the ordinary citizen of that country experiences on an everyday occurrence, you probably didn't see the whole picture of that country. Unless you have to work with people first-hand to learn about their local and governmental rules and regulations, or see the kickbacks and payoffs to complete almost anything constructive, you haven't the foggiest idea about that country.

In order to be successful in the international markets, it was important to learn as much about their cultures as possible. I took in all the experiences expounded by my IBG coworkers, and did a lot of reading about the various countries we served, especially if I was planning to travel there soon.

I probably should have taken more time to see some touristy stuff, but with a growing family at home, trips away from home were difficult by itself, not to mention some of the situations I found myself in while working overseas.

During my travels over those four years in the IBG, I got to meet and become friends with many people from many countries. Even today, I keep in regular contact with several of them via Facebook, emails, letters, Skype and even sometimes I am surprised with a Christmas Eve phone call from one or more of them. The many long discussions with these friends usually involved them warning me of what might happen to the USA if similar things happen as they have experienced over the years. I never knew how much almost every nation depends on the USA economy, until I traveled there to work with them. Some warned me of an evil master plan that already gobbled them up, and heading our way to the USA. Of course, if I tell my friends that, I would be labeled as either crazy or a radical.

In the mid-90's, America got gobbled! The subject of this so-called globalization that was supposed to be so good for us was starting to take a big chunk out of us. During the mid-90's, our government caved into signing as many free trade agreements as they could. It didn't take an economist or a rocket scientist to realize that our jobs would soon be vacating our land at a record pace beginning then. It was often said years before that time that there were almost not enough jobs to employ both women and men here in the USA, and that plight became a reality during the time our jobs were being exported. I have nothing against jobs or equal opportunities for both men and woman, but gasp at what our leaders did to create a divide in the workplace with the loss of so many jobs. The number of haves and have-nots increased almost overnight.

As the world broadens its technological advancements in manufacturing, it was clear that less and less people would be required to make the same amount of goods. People were replaced by automation leaving only the service industry the ability for growth. That ended when telecommunications grew to a point where our inquiries could be answered by someone in India upon calling a toll-free phone number. Now our service industry jobs were being shipped off overseas, leaving us with fewer and fewer jobs here in the States.

Farming was one of our last footholds in the economy. But the advancements of farm and construction equipment, and the need to broaden company's sales regions, brought the ability for third world countries to cultivate, plant, fertilize and grow their own food crops. Also, the road building technologies expanded resources in these same third world regions to make sure the farmers there could get their products to markets. After all, you can teach and demonstrate to other countries how to work their land and become successful crop growers, but if there isn't an infrastructure to get the product into a supply chain, all the demonstrations are useless. Unfortunately, I and the company I worked for were part of the reason our crop exports have fallen so drastically in the past decade.

Juan, a crane operator in the Ciudad Guyana, Venezuela, presented me with a craft-made rendition of a native Venezuelan bow and arrow. I wondered how I would get it through airport security, but Juan had a solution for that too. He took small needle-nosed pliers and rolled up the arrow tip. He instructed me to unroll it when I got home, which I did, and hung onto that gift for many years. Jacek from Poland presented me with a copy of an old warrior's hatchet. This hatchet was about 3.5 feet long and just barely fit into my large suitcase diagonally. No problems through security or customs then, but I bet neither of these quasi weapons would clear any airport security these days.

Being the IBG Product Support Manager and having some very excellent Field Service Engineers and Product Sales Managers to work with, I could choose my own travel schedule to coincide with most of my children's "growing up" activities. I always took a three week trip between basketball and baseball seasons. Because there are religious holidays until the end of February, that trip would usually consist of a pilgrimage through Asia and then on to Australia. The transition between those two countries was always tough. I usually spent the last day in Asia visiting some customers and our dealer in the Kuala Lumpur area, doing my job in the hot, humid Malaysian sun, before getting back to the airport in Singapore to catch my overnight flight to Sydney, where my bright-eyed friend, Denis, would pick me up at the airport at about 7 AM and drive me directly to their group office without any chance for sleep from a couple of nights ago. Denis always had some sales or service gimmick he was promoting that he wanted input into or wanted assistance putting it together for a sales meeting the next day, so there was little time for sleep. There was little time to relax.

I could never sleep on an airplane. My height of 6'2" was just too tall to comfortably rest my head on the backrest and try to sleep. As I usually had an aisle seat, someone was always bumping my arm, thus making it difficult to get any shut eye on the plane. But I do remember one Asian trip flying back from Seoul, South Korea, where I took a window seat, leaned against it, and fell asleep before we took off from Seoul. When I was awakened by the flight attendant in San Francisco, I was shocked when I realized where we were and that everyone else had exited the plane already. As I exited the plane with the stewardess, we met an emergency crew approaching the door of the aircraft, and I heard her tell them that I was okay and that I was just asleep. That was the trip that I must have overdosed on kimchi, a spicy pickled or fermented mixture containing cabbage, onions, and sometimes fish, variously seasoned with garlic, horseradish, red peppers, and ginger, (according to the online dictionary). I devoured it a couple times a day while in S. Korea. Cindy still reminds me not to poison my system with that stuff, as she claims I smelled like garlic for a week after my return, not to mention that the mattress and my pillow would never smell the same again. I also enjoyed eel prepared on a table-mounted charcoal grill. When telling the dealer manager that I really enjoyed both the local eel and kimchi, he planned a dinner with everyone in his dealership on my last night there. Guess what we had for dinner...grilled eel and kimchi, and plenty of beverages.

I was visiting a customer in the city of Yantai, up in the northeastern parts of China. On the first night, it was always customary to meet with the customer for dinner and drinks. It was also customary in those parts, that the guest could choose their beverage of choice. Everyone there would also drink the same chosen drink. On the flight to Yantai on China Eastern Airlines, I saw a magazine ad for a beer made in Yantai. So when asked what I wanted to drink, I proclaimed that I wanted to try some of their locally brewed, Yantai Beer. I chose beer, because I didn't want to get caught up with any of their customary fire-water, something that I didn't have much appetite for, plus I had to be able to perform for the customer the next day. Our local sales rep had reserved a private dining room at a nice restaurant, a round table with a huge Lazy Susan centered on top of the table. There were about 8 or 10 people from our company and the customer's, and the beer started flowing. One of the customer's men raised his glass and said something in Chinese as he lifted his glass full of beer towards me. Our company rep told he was telling me the equivalent of "kampai" or cheers, or bottoms-up. The beer drinking session had begun. I had to chug an eight ounce glass of beer with everyone at the table, one at a time. I had a waiter standing next to me at all times to keep my glass in full order ready for the next toast. When it came time to toast with my counterpart from the customer's company, he challenged me to doing it twice with him in rapid order. By the time dinner was celebrated, our company rep had counted 28 empty two liter bottles sitting in the corner of the room, and one person's head resting squarely in the center of his dinner plate, fast asleep…but it wasn't mine.

At the same dinner, I was asked what I want to eat, and I jumped at the word, "seafood", as we were only a stone's throw away from the East China Sea. I think we were served everything and anything that ever slithered, crawled or even came close to the ocean. I couldn't tell you much of what was served that night, but I had enough beer in me to consume it all. As the family style food was being presented to me on the Lazy Susan on the table, everyone made sure I had the first try at all of the dishes, and there were at least twenty various dishes served. I recognized when something really weird was placed in front of me as everyone would stop what they were doing and watch intently to see how the Yankee would take to liking the morsels of unknown. On one particular dish, I had about 22 eyes (also counting the beer servers and waiter) staring me down. This really must have been something weird! I think they thought I was an alright type of guy when I tasted it and rolled back the Lazy Susan and took some more of whatever it was. Man, the things one has to do to appease customers in the world! I think I still have a picture of that dinner and the empty beer bottles sitting in the corner somewhere here in the house. Maybe when I find those pictures, I'll also find that photo for Tom B that contained our ill-fitting baseball pants.

My international travel days extended from 1978 to 2008. I haven't been on an airplane since, and for some reason, I do not miss it. But now I sit back, reflect and think about all I have learned and put the big puzzle together that remains jumbled inside my head.

There are times I wish not to reflect on things because I know the outcome is not going to be good. I pray for our nation's sake that I am wrong.

Chapter Five

Notions

I was reading an article in our beloved local newspaper. I usually take any political article with a grain of salt, because our McClatchy owned newspaper is filled with left wing propaganda, as are most newspapers and TV stations these days, but this one intrigued me more than most. It invited investigation. Even way back into the late 1990's, there was a great deal of information available on the internet, not nearly as much as today, but adequate for the times.

The nicely written article tried not to persuade anyone of any political stance or tried to demonize anyone. The article quietly opened my eyes by inviting me to do some of my own investigative work in determining exactly what was going on in America.

Bill Clinton seemed to have the nation's economy humming in his second term. Unemployment was relatively low and most people seemed to be happy. But the control of the duck swimming on top of the water usually doesn't reveal all the hidden work below the surface.

The article referred its readers to a document published as the Communist Party Goals, entered into the Congressional records in 1963. The article warned people to watch for advancement in these once lofty goals, but their movement should be considered not on the "Dead on Arrival" shortlist, but as a working document in today's American society going forward.

Bill Ayer's underground society movements of the 60's and early 70's was not at all dead, and when all is considered, that movement has gathered strength and a grip on our nation's people.

I took the opportunity several times since reading that article to find more and more evidence that the Communist Socialist movement is alive and well and moving towards complete domination in our country.

Here is a copy of that Congressional report, documented in January of 1963:

United States Communist Party Goals (1963)

Documention below Congressional Record--Appendix, pp. A34-A35January 10, 1963Current Communist Goals
EXTENSION OF REMARKS OF HON. A. S. HERLONG, JR.OF FLORIDA IN THE HOUSE OF REPRESENTATIVES
Thursday, January 10, 1963
Mr. HERLONG. Mr. Speaker, Mrs. Patricia Nordman of De Land, Fla., is an ardent and articulate opponent of communism, and until recently published the De Land Courier, which she dedicated to the purpose of alerting the public to the dangers of communism in America. At Mrs. Nordman's request, I include in the RECORD, under unanimous consent, the following" Current Communist Goals," which she identifies as an excerpt from "The Naked Communist," by Cleon Skousen: From "The Naked Communist," by Cleon Skousen]

CURRENT COMMUNIST GOALS [1]

1. U.S. acceptance of coexistence as the only alternative to atomic war.
2. U.S. willingness to capitulate in preference to engaging in atomic war.
3. Develop the illusion that total disarmament [by] the United States would be a demonstration of moral strength.

---

[1] http://www.freerepublic.com/focus/f-news/1595013/posts

*4. Permit free trade between all nations regardless of Communist affiliation and regardless of whether or not items could be used for war.

5. Extension of long-term loans to Russia and Soviet satellites.

*6. Provide American aid to all nations regardless of Communist domination.

7. Grant recognition of Red China. Admission of Red China to the U.N.

8. Set up East and West Germany as separate states in spite of Khrushchev's promise in 1955 to settle the German question by free elections under supervision of the U.N.

*9. Prolong the conferences to ban atomic tests because the United States has agreed to suspend tests as long as negotiations are in progress.

*10. Allow all Soviet satellites individual representation in the U.N.

*11. Promote the U.N. as the only hope for mankind. If its charter is rewritten, demand that it be set up as a one-world government with its own independent armed forces. (Some Communist leaders believe the world can be taken over as easily by the U.N. as by Moscow. Sometimes these two centers compete with each other as they are now doing in the Congo.)

*12. Resist any attempt to outlaw the Communist Party.

13. Do away with all loyalty oaths.

14. Continue giving Russia access to the U.S. Patent Office.

*15. Capture one or both of the political parties in the United States.

*16. Use technical decisions of the courts to weaken basic American institutions by claiming their activities violate civil rights.

*17. Get control of the schools. Use them as transmission belts for socialism and current Communist propaganda. Soften the curriculum. Get control of teachers' associations. Put the party line in textbooks.

*18. Gain control of all student newspapers.

*19. Use student riots to foment public protests against programs or organizations which are under Communist attack.

*20. Infiltrate the press. Get control of book-review assignments, editorial writing, and policy making positions.

*21. Gain control of key positions in radio, TV, and motion pictures.

*22. Continue discrediting American culture by degrading all forms of artistic expression. An American Communist cell was told to "eliminate all good sculpture from parks and buildings, substitute shapeless, awkward and meaningless forms."

*23. Control art critics and directors of art museums. "Our plan is to promote ugliness, repulsive, meaningless art."

*24. Eliminate all laws governing obscenity by calling them "censorship" and a violation of free speech and free press.

*25. Break down cultural standards of morality by promoting pornography and obscenity in books, magazines, motion pictures, radio, and TV.

*26. Present homosexuality, degeneracy and promiscuity as "normal, natural, & healthy."

*27. Infiltrate the churches and replace revealed religion with "social" religion. Discredit the Bible and emphasize the need for intellectual maturity which does not need a "religious crutch."

*28. Eliminate prayer or any phase of religious expression in the schools on the ground that it violates the principle of "separation of church and state."

*29. Discredit the American Constitution by calling it inadequate, old-fashioned, out of step with modern needs, a hindrance to cooperation between nations on a worldwide basis.

*30. Discredit the American Founding Fathers. Present them as selfish aristocrats who had no concern for the "common man."

*31. Belittle all forms of American culture and discourage the teaching of American history on the ground that it was *only a minor part of the "big picture." Give more emphasis to Russian history since the Communists took over.*

32. Support any socialist movement to give centralized control over any part of the culture--education, social agencies, welfare programs, mental health clinics, etc.

33. Eliminate all laws or procedures which interfere with the operation of the Communist apparatus.

34. Eliminate the House Committee on Un-American Activities.

35. Discredit and eventually dismantle the FBI.

36. Infiltrate and gain control of more unions.

37. Infiltrate and gain control of big business.

38. Transfer some of the powers of arrest from the police to social agencies. Treat all behavioral problems as psychiatric disorders which no one but psychiatrists can understand [or treat].

39. Dominate the psychiatric profession and use mental health laws as a means of gaining coercive control over those who oppose Communist goals.

40. Discredit the family as an institution. Encourage promiscuity and easy divorce.

41. Emphasize the need to raise children away from the negative influence of parents. Attribute prejudices, mental blocks and retarding of children to suppressive influence of parents.

42. Create the impression that violence and insurrection are legitimate aspects of the American tradition; that students and special-interest groups should rise up and use "united force" to solve economic, political or social problems.

43. Overthrow all colonial governments before native populations are ready for self-government.

44. Internationalize the Panama Canal.

45. Repeal the Connally reservation so the United States cannot prevent the World Court from seizing jurisdiction over domestic problems. Give the World Court jurisdiction over nations and individuals alike.

* = Line items above that I believe have been recently completed or are proactively being pursued.

Wow, if our grandparents could see us now! Talk about long term planning? Remember that discussion in an earlier chapter of the book?

How can a nation so brave, so free, so rich in intellectual people and property fall prey to these terms and pretenses? Have our successes lulled us into a republic of naivety?

Chapter Five

Warnings

I was sitting in the airport in Singapore in 2004, waiting for United Airline to get their "you-know-what" together for the flight home to America. During my short five year position with the International Business Group of our 23000 employee company, I was a frequent traveler in high regards on many airlines. I adventure to say that when my stint with our company's IBG broke up in 1995, there were several airlines that thought I must have died. In 2011, I used up the last of my frequent flyer miles on some hotel rooms on a trip taken with my wife. Being from the upper Midwest, I amassed a huge amount of frequent flyer miles with Northwest Airlines, enough, in fact, that I was able to schedule a trip for my entire family to Singapore in 1995. Some miles expired, some airlines went out of business or merged with someone else since, but I enjoyed some of the miles even if it was for a free hotel room for me and my family here and there.

Back to Singapore......I encountered a strange discussion with a gentleman that I learned was a world history buff from Jakarta, Indonesia. He was a Professor of Modern Civilizations at one of the local universities near or in Jakarta. During our almost one hour discussion, he spoke of why he thought the Socialists were finally winning the war with America. His premise was that although America seemed naïve enough to believe they broke the back of Communism when the Berlin Wall was toppled, we should not be surprised if we will someday wake up and find ourselves in an un-reversible position with them. He explained that he believed that if we are to win the fight against Communism, we would have to stand tight to our founding beliefs, and not sway towards their oppression. As the discussion continued I wasn't sure which side he was taking or if there was a side to be taken. I had hoped to talk to him some more in our next stop in

Tokyo, but with the lateness our flight, we never did have a chance to talk again.

It was during that trip that I started to assemble my thoughts of our American direction, and pieced together some experiences that have haunted me for quite a while. In 1969, as a freshman at the University of Wisconsin, Stevens Point, a dormitory friend and I attended a rally at the student union where a character named Bill Ayers, was the lead guest (of honor). Bill Ayers was making the college campus circuit pushing his ideological thoughts on students. Although I didn't agree with much he was saying, especially when he tried to promote breaking up children from their parents for what he called "for obvious reasons", I listened intently. About six months later, I read that Ayers was charged in connection with a New York City building bomb explosion. We never saw him again on our campus, although some yocal-locals who had teamed up for his cause were often seen around our university grounds holding up signs and chanting obscure things that I didn't always agree with. I didn't think much more of it, and found some sport and even some occasional trout fishing in the area to surround the time that I should have been studying.

The Weather Underground, they called it. Didn't make much sense of it then but slowly pieced together their directions and ambitions since then.

Chapter Six

Under the Weather

One time in 2005, while doing an exercise walk on our subdivision's paths, I got the crazy idea to jog a little ways. I normally settled for a very brisk paced walk for exercise, as I didn't want to interject all that stress on my knees from my somewhat over proportioned body mass. But today, feeling good, I decided to add a little jogging. I picked a starting point about three blocks from my home, and decided that I would kick it in gear when I got to that point.

As I reached the point of the start of the run, I sprang into action. If there was a crowd watching, they probably wouldn't have seen much difference between my fast walk and my slow run. This phenomenon is often witnessed as I often passed up joggers when I was walking. It was on about my tenth jogging step that my right knee seemed to give out. Luckily, I was close to the right edge of the path and fell on the edge of the grass next to the pathway. Looking around to see if anyone saw me, and seeing no one, I dusted off my pride, got up and continued to walk the rest of the way home.

A couple of months later, I was descending from one of the remote office trailer on a jobsite. On the second of three steps, my knee again gave way, this time there was pain as I scrapped my knees into the hard, hot blacktop surface below. What the hell? I know I'm a big guy. I know I probably should be losing some weight and or not spending so much time behind a desk at work, but c'mon man, this isn't right. Something is wrong.

My baseball, basketball playing son received a workout gym contraption several years ago for his birthday. It was one made by Weider that had several workout stations on it. Because I realized something was amiss with my legs, I would as a daily routine go down into our basement and do 100 leg presses, followed up by upper body workouts. After 3 or four months of almost a daily regiment on that gym set, I should be feeling stronger, but I didn't. I increased the weights a little thinking that would help, but it didn't. If anything, I was feeling a little weaker in my legs, and arms. I also noticed that I was losing some gripping strength in my left hand.

I spent the months of November, December, 2006 and January of 2007 in our corporate office working in a War Room set up for about 8 employees to ardently work on a huge bid for the Tank and Army Command (TACOM). I had been involved with TACOM on one other occasion when I had to visit Warren, MI and sit down with government personnel on some cranes that they had purchased about 10 years before. It was reported that some of the soldier crane operators were tipping our cranes over while they lifted a load over the rated capacity of the crane. They requested a presentation to tell them how to avoid such a happening. My job was to nicely communicate the correct operation of the crane so as not to tip it over. My challenge was to nicely but firmly suggest that they know the approximate weight of the article being lifted, and review the Lift capability Chart affixed in each crane that listed the maximum working radius for lifting that weight. I remember entering the huge office complex and witnessed a room full of office desks, maybe around 40 of them. I also noticed that about half the people sitting at the desks had their heads down on the desk, presumably taking a nap. Once in the conference room, it was evident that the message that I was tasked to give them had to travel down a long chain of command to reach the operators of the cranes. Upon leaving the conference room after the hour long session, I again witness the workers at the desks with their heads down, sleeping. A very sad example of the government worker!

While working those months in the War Room, I found it more and more difficult to get up from a seated position. I had to have the adjoining chairs situated just right to be able to get up. The bid was due the first week in February, and I was part of most of it, including writing the first product definition to be used by TACOM for the product being bid.

My fingers started to stiffen up some more, almost arthritic like. They didn't want to bend when I wanted them to, and I found it more and more difficult to pull open things, like a drawer, or the dishwasher with my fingertips. My hand, arm and leg strength was leaving me.

During my next visit to my doctor, I told him about my situation and he referred me to an orthopedic specialist. The first possible conclusion from the first of three specialists was that I possibly had the start of carpal tunnel syndrome, which was a problem in the wrist area where the nerves and tendons for the fingers run. They conducted an EMG (electromyogram), which was a different experience for me. They insert electric probes on different parts of your body, then measure the lapse time between the two points while sending an electric shock. My first EMG did show some irregularities, so I was referred to another orthopedic specialist who decided to check my neck area out with another EMG. So, let's just place those probes on different parts of the body and do some more measuring...... That test was also inconclusive, so I was referred to another specialist in the same clinic for another appointment. As I left the clinic that day, I peered at the list of orthopedic specialists in that clinic, and now realized that I still hadn't seen more than half the specialist on the list, if I was to be referred to them all......
After seeing the third specialist and still not have heard any news, good or bad, I was referred to a neurologist at another clinic. Two weeks later, I was at his office, repeating the same EMG tests that had been done before, but this time, he insisted on some special blood tests. He told me to come back in a week for his diagnosis.

For some reason, I was thinking that this doctor may be able to tell me why my muscles were diminishing. During that time I imagined everything from having a deadly virus inside me eating up my muscles to a reaction from some lawn chemicals that I had been using every year, or something deadly that I ate in China. It was a long week in my life.

I'm not sure if I was relived or saddened by his diagnosis. The doctor walked into the sterile examination room and pulled up his chair to a position right in front of me. He clasped a single sheet of paper that I could see was printed off the internet. Wait a minute....was I going to get an internet diagnosis here? I certainly hope not. He calmly looked into my eyes and said, "Mr. King, I believe you have a very rare form of Muscular Dystrophy, called Inclusion Body Myositis. The good news is that you probably won't die from it. The bad news is that there is no known medication that will help this condition. It's unknown what causes this condition."

I lowered my eyes and again peered at the single sheet of paper in his hand. "I printed off this sheet from the internet so you knew of a good website to read more about your condition and its pending outlook."

I left the doctor's office kind of relieved we had a diagnosis, but the anxiety within me questioned the reality of it all. Why me? A couple of months later, I had a muscle biopsy performed, the sample sent to Mayo Clinic and the diagnosis of IBM was verified.

Wikipedia explains this disease as follows:

Inclusion body myositis (IBM) is an inflammatory muscle disease, characterized by slowly progressive weakness and wasting of both distal and proximal muscles, most apparent in the muscles of the arms and legs. There are two types: sporadic inclusion body myositis (sIBM) and hereditary inclusion body myopathy (hIBM).

In sporadic inclusion body myositis [MY-oh-sigh-tis] muscle, two processes, one autoimmune and the other degenerative, appear to occur in the muscle cells in parallel. The inflammation aspect is characterized by the cloning of T cells that appear to be driven by specific antigens to invade muscle fibers. The degeneration aspect is characterized by the appearance of holes in the muscle cell vacuoles, deposits of abnormal proteins within the cells and in filamentous inclusions (hence the name inclusion body myositis).

sIBM is a rare yet increasingly prevalent disease, being the most common cause of inflammatory myopathy in the over 50s; the most recent research, done in Australia, indicates that the incidence of IBM varies and is different in different populations and different ethnic groups. The authors found that the current prevalence was 14.9 per million in the overall population, with a prevalence of 51.3 per million population in people over 50 years of age. As seen in these numbers, sIBM is an age-related disease – its incidence increases with age and symptoms usually begin after 50 years of age. It is the most common acquired muscle disorder seen in people over 50, although about 20% of cases display symptoms before the age of 50. Weakness comes on slowly (over months or years) and progresses steadily and usually leads to severe weakness and wasting of arm and leg muscles. It is slightly more common in men than women. Patients may become unable to perform daily living activities and most require assistive devices within 5 to 10 years of symptom onset. sIBM is not considered a fatal disorder – barring complications, all things being equal, sIBM will not kill (but the risk of serious injury due to falls is increased).[2]

There are many other definitions of the disease, but they all primarily say the same thing……cause unknown, no meds defined for it, no cure identified.

Only two days after learning about my diagnosis, another tragedy struck. I was laid off from my job after 34.5 years

---

[2] http://en.wikipedia.org/wiki/Inclusion_body_myositis

with the same company. This was not a good week for me or my family. This was in March of 2007. By the way, TACOM announced our winning the bid for the large equipment sale in April, about a month after being let go. We had won a bid for more than $180 million over the next ten years.

My arms and hands were getting so weak, that I had to ask a coworker to carry the box of my personal belongings out from my office desk to my vehicle.

By this time I could visually see the atrophy on my upper arms and upper legs. My fingers were escaping any serious work ability. If the good Lord wouldn't have built man with his thumb opposite his other fingers, I wouldn't be able to pick up anything.

One hundred gazillion things were racing through my mind. How would I get another job? Would I be able to get another job? How will I support my family?

I was 55 and decided on retirement in September 2007, and filed for SSI Disability, which I was granted about 5 months later. Two years from the date of my SSI Disability, I would be eligible for Medicare, something I had planned on not using for another 8 or 10 years.

I hear so many people complain about how hard it is to get on SSI Disability. I also see a lot of lawyer's ads on TV begging to help people who have not been refused SSI Disability before they are of age. I did not utilize a lawyer, what I did do was offer as much information as possible to the SSI Disability office via the signup request sheets on SSI's website. I guess I looked at it this way.....if you give them enough information to make their decision easy, the chances of getting accepted on the first attempt greatly increases. If you offer only a basic amount of info and make the claim officer's life more difficult, chances are your request will end up in the "rejected" file. When they asked for medical history, I put the effort in to give them a complete synopsis of my recent medical history. When they asked for doctor's names addresses and phone numbers, I gave them all that info. I didn't want to give even the laziest of claim officers any reason to deny my request. I figure all the time I spent making my request full and accurate was well worth the $5,800 the lawyers charge to do the same task.

The last step in the process was with a SSI appointed physician for an exam and consultation. When I checked in at the front desk, I was told to have a seat and they would be right with me. I responded by stating that there were no chairs in the waiting room that I could use and be able to stand back up again, so I stood near the magazine rack for about 5 minutes until I was called into the room. When the physician came into the room, I was still standing, and he politely offered me the empty chair in the room. I declined, and told him that I needed a chair at least 24" in height to be able to stand up from. He promptly wrote that in his notes. He then asked me to bend my back forward, which I did without problem before asking me to bend my knees and see how far down I could go. I bent my knees just a few inches before I asked the doc how many strong people he had on staff, because it would take a few very strong people to scrape me off the floor when I fell, and I could tell him that I was getting close to that point. He instructed me not to fall, and again started writing things in his report. He looked at my prior history and saw reports from my neurologists, and results of my muscle biopsy from the Mayo Clinic and MDA Clinic notes.

When asked about my work history, I was sure to tell him that I was laid off two days after being diagnosed with Inclusion Body Myositis. He confessed that he knew nothing of that disease. I gave him a brief layman's description of IBM, and he proceeded to again do a lot of writing on the paper form in front of him. He didn't give me any indication what his general conclusion was before I left his office. I was probably the only patient he ever had that stood through the whole exam and consultation. Now, some more waiting until I heard from the SSI office.

About five months after first applying for SSI Disability, I received notification of acceptance with their official date of disability as two weeks after I had been laid off in 2007. I always complained about paying into Social Security during my 34 year career, but rescind all those comments, because now I was using that insurance as it was design.

If someone would come up with an IBM cure tomorrow, I would not benefit from it. Once muscle tissue is taken by atrophy, it is not going to come back.

Chapter Seven

Everyone's Moving On

Life is too short to show too much self-pity, it's time to move on with my life despite my uncertain future. I got what I got, no one can say why, no one can say how fast it will consume my body.

I spend my days planning. It's a good thing I had all that product planning and support experience in my years on the job. Everyone periodically thinks about End of Life planning. People think about making their wills, when to announce a DNR (Do Not Resuscitate), and burial intentions. My end of life planning extended itself into early thoughts of things like, "How will I get up out of bed when my legs and arms have no strength at all"; "Will I soon be on a catheter and urinate into a bag", "Have I purchase the right transfer board"? "Will my wife be able to care for me or am I destined for a care home", etc.

I have plenty of time to think about things. I also have plenty of time to think about my Grandchildren's futures. What's changing these days that will stifle their futures? What's going on in America? What's up with our government's leaders?

The 2008, 2010 & 2012 national elections really intrigued me. Although I wasn't particularly happy with the second term of George W., I was even more pessimistic of the new Democratic choice for President. I needed to learn more about him before I voted, but the necessary info to make an intelligent choice was not made available. So, I voted for what seemed to be the least of two evils, John McCain.

I'm not sure there were enough people in the USA who thought it was weird that there was no or little info about the new Chicagoan running for the highest position in our country. Upon searching for information, I learned that I could get more info that was available on our city's dog catcher than I could on this presidential candidate. I think he must have misunderstood the ballot as saying "White House Residential Candidate" instead of "White House Presidential Candidate". No concrete facts were made available on any of the network news shows, although all sung his praise to the highest heavens. All we were told was that he had some Chicago community organizing experience, and then a couple of introductory years in the US Senate…… but spent most of that time campaigning, and that made him qualified?

Just shortly after the 2008 election and the election of Barack Hussein Obama into the White House, I recalled my conversation with the Indonesian Professor and my experience listening to Bill Ayers back in my college days. I learned that Obama's campaign manager was affiliated with the Communist Party a few years back, and learned that Barack Obama has announced his intention to run for President at the home of Bill Ayers. Upon doing a little more reading on the subject, our newly elected President had plenty of ties to the old Communist Party, but did not freely divulge it during his campaigning. Low and behold, his mother was from the very city that I now live in, Wichita, Ks, and had ties to the Communist Party here years ago. His birth father had strong Communist Party ties; his step-father could be readily traced to the Communist Party in Indonesia, where Barack lived for a few years. Obama lived with his grandparents in Hawaii who were strong supporters of the Communist Party and Obama himself had strong ties to the Communist Party before, during and after his college days, and in fact held a prominent position within a Communist party group in Illinois in the 90's. No wonder his past was sealed off from the public.

Why wasn't the press all over this?

Going back to the old Communist Party Goals published in 1963 is the answer to that question. Remember goals # 20 and 21: *Infiltrate the press;* and *Gain control of key positions in radio, TV, and motion pictures.* Senator Obama did not make that happen. Community Organizer Obama didn't make that happen. Lawyer Obama did not make that happen. All of that work was completed by some very long term planning and execution of a Communist Party Business plan to overtake the USA........just as they originally wanted to do back 40-50 years ago.

Goal number 15: *Capture one or both of the political parties in the United States.* Bingo! They had been working on it for many years, but they could actually say they captured the Democratic Party's flag by the late 1980's. The only thing left was to find and train the right candidate, and all that took was to look into their party ranks and identify Barack Obama for the task of officially turning the Communist Party into the presidency of the United States of America. That task was completed in November of 2008.

I was just listening to the President give one of his canned State of the Union Addresses. He promised us the earth and the moon again and directly told us it wouldn't cost us "one dime". Here's an example of the type of true lies a communist politician will tell all his gullible followers. I agree... it won't cost us "one dime". It will cost us millions or billions of dimes. I wonder how many people picked up on that.

Chapter Eight

Volt Shocked

Gas prices really soared near the start of the second decade of the new millennium and car manufacturers held out their hands towards the government asking for taxpayer's dimes to float their energy savings projects. How many dimes actually were invested into the creation of energy-efficient automobiles is anyone's guess, but a classic mistake was brewing in the halls of General Motors. When it was announced that GM was going to introduce their energy efficient piece of technology under the Chevrolet badge, I was puzzled and bewildered.

My years in the Product Support field often lent myself to being the buffer between Engineering and Manufacturing. The engineer's ideas were often too good for the cost consciousness of manufacturing, and the cost of manufacturing ultimately affected the price of the product to the consumer. If the cost to the consumer is too high, only a limited amount of high end consumers would purchase your product.

So what did GM do with their expensive alternative to the gas-only automobile? They opted to target the lower and middle class with a car priced higher than they could afford. I'm sorry, but rich people don't purchase many Chevrolets. Their egos won't allow it. So why build an overpriced car for a class of people who can't afford it? Why not pick your Cadillac badge to hang on your new invention if you want to sell to the upper class? If GM was successful in selling the car to the rich under the Cadillac badge, they could then de-option it for the Chevy type of people. I know this rhetoric sounds a lot like some class warfare, but marketing is marketing and GM missed their mark in this category. I wonder how many GM VP's bought into this decision?

Who in their right mind would pay way too much money for a car that can only go 35 miles between charges (before the gas kicks in)? I'm not sure because I have no data to back this up, but I bet the average commute for an average working in a large city is more than 35 miles.

Gasoline powered cars are going to be here for a while, so car manufacturers had better find a way to make them more energy efficient, and the government better get off their asses and allow the US to capitalize on the vast amounts of fossil fuels available under our own soils.

Oil makes the world go 'round. By result of their own current policies, our White House will probably get us into more wars than they intend to get us out of. We only have one friend left in the oil producing lands of the Middle East, and they don't produce an overabundance of oil that they can sell to us. We have accepted high gasoline prices as the new normal, and people are starting to call $3.25 a gallon, cheap gasoline. I guess we fell into another trap, didn't we? Us, poor gullible US citizens…..

Chapter Nine

Flashback

My Uncle Erv died in 2007. He had quit farming several years prior because of his age and health, but still remained living on the old family homestead. The old farmhouse was getting a bit drafty, and the old gravity wood-fired furnace originally installed in 1932 that consumed most of the dark and dingy basement had been replaced with a more modern type of heating system.

My just retired cousin Jim and his wife took over the old homestead, and immediately built a new home behind the old farm house. After they moved into their new dwelling, Jim hired a company to come and demolish the old farm house. Within an hour or two, the base for quite a few memories came crashing down and all that was left was were the photos that Jim took during the demolition.

The farmhouse sat up on a large hill where the distant view was amazing. When I was young, I swear you could see the whole world from the second story of the old farmhouse. To the west of the house across a field sat a small patch of woods that faced the second story bedroom I slept in during my younger days working my summers on the farm. At night this small woods adorned the evening air with the sounds of a couple of Whip-poor-will birds romancing each other. The nighttime view out the second story window in the non-air-conditioned house was sometimes interrupted by the flashes of hundreds of lightning bugs illuminating the night sky. Occasionally, we would spot a deer crossing one of open fields under the moon-lit sky.

The old dairy barn still sits in its place, although Jim tells me he has some concerns about the structural integrity of it, and probably won't be able to insure it much longer. During my last visit to the now empty barn, I recalled lots of sweat spread inside this barn. Luckily most of it was on the top floor where the hay was stored and less sweat equity in the lower level where the dairy cows were milked. That didn't mean that I missed my opportunities to feed the cows and clean the livestock pens. During the haying season, the hot place to be was up in the hay mow, about 40 feet up from the floor of the barn. When the side of the barn we were storing hay on reached the top near the apex of the barn roof, we were probably 50 feet above the barn floor. I sure am glad Uncle Erv had made that hay bale elevator to reach to the top.

Picture of the King Farm in 1982

One time during haying season, I lost my wallet while driving the tractor pulling the baler and hay wagon. Upon realizing it had worked its way out of my pocket seat on the roundish shaped International Harvester tractor seat, Tom and I spent about an hour walking the already cut and harvested field looking for my wallet. I think I only had about $20 dollars in it at the time, but I also had my Wisconsin driving learner's permit in it, and of course, I couldn't lose that! Giving up my search, we had fallen behind towing the loaded hay wagon to the barn, so I jump on one of the utility tractors and pulled the loaded wagon to the barn for unloading. As it was my turn up in the hay mow, I jumped off the tractor and raced up the ladder. As we were about half done with the load, my cousin Tom was putting the bales from the wagon on the elevator a little faster than I could take them off and pile them. If you ever have been in a hay mow working with the 18" x 36" x 14" bales weighing approximately 65 lbs., and secured with two pieces of machine-tied baler twine, you probably can realize that each bale contains two trip hazards each when walking on them. Well, I tripped on one and fell down making my attempt to keep up with the bales a little more difficult. By the time I reached the area where the bales came off the elevator extension, two bales had already fallen off. When the second bale fell off the elevator extension, it rolled off the previous bale and rolled over. Nestled sweetly underneath one of the bales twines was my wallet. I quickly pulled it out from underneath the bale twine and put it in my pocket, as more hay bales were on their way up the elevator. After we had finish that load, I descended the ladder from the mow, and pulled the wallet out of my pocket to show Tom who had helped me search the field for it. To our amazement, the only damage to the wallet was that a small piece of the corner had been clipped off presumably by the feed cutter on the baler. What luck!

The smell of the fresh air coming into the farmhouse in my younger days was only interrupted by the memory of Grandma King making fresh bread in the early hours of the morning. Bread was a main staple in the farm house and Grandma King would always be baking something on her old cook stove. She used to bake nine loaves of bread in the wood oven in the stove. She made a version of bread that was excellent. It used raw boiled milk that was then chilled with an active yeast, and water leftover from boiling potatoes. During harvest season, she made bread every day.

I'm not sure if nine loaves is what fit into the oven at one time or if that was the number of pans it took to fit her normal recipe amounts. But none the less, warm homemade bread was always welcomed at the morning breakfast table on the farm, or any meal thereafter.

An apple orchard sat just on the west side of the house, with plenty of good apples to munch on during the fall. Again, there were apple pies made from fresh apples as well as ones from apples that were canned or frozen for later use.

When I was young Christmas was always celebrated at Grandma's house on the family farm. We would get up early in the morning at our own homes, open our gifts just like all kids do, then it was off to church, then on to the farm. Christmas was always fun because it was a time when all the aunts, uncles and cousins would get together and have some great times. I'm sure the large crowd taxed Grandma's kitchen to the max, and the old Kelvinator refrigerator couldn't hold all the goods required for such a crowd, so there were a few boxes out on a couch in the unheated, but enclosed porch. It was Wisconsin, not need to worry about spoilage of the food to be prepared as long as the collie, named Laddie, kept her nose out of it.

In my younger years, I vaguely remember there were two horses on the farm named Mack and Prince. They would use them less as tractors were beginning to take over most chores requiring brute strength. Mack and Price were Percherons, primarily used as work horses. I remember the two beasts pulling large logs out of the woods at the farm during firewood collecting weekends. One of the horses was considered gentle, but the other was considered feisty and often would try to nip any stranger within its reach. I remember my uncle offering me a ride on the back of the feisty horse on the way back to the woods to get another log. When I objected to being placed on the "mean" horse, he explained if I were on the back of the nice horse, the mean hose could reach to try and bite me. I accepted that, but was apprehensive about the situation until I was removed from his back. I guess sometimes you have to sit on evil's back to keep from being bitten by it.

I remember accidently wrecking my family's Christmas one year. Me and my cousins were outside playing in the cold and snow and were called in for Christmas dinner. The sound of someone's voice beckoning us for Christmas dinner sent us all rushing to the farmhouse door. I slipped on some ice near the door and fell landing on a boot scrapper sitting just to the right of the left hinged door. It was my head that hit the boot scrapper, and a nice gash on the lower part of my forehead centered right above my eyes produced more blood that I was used to seeing even during pig butchering sessions. Not good. Instead of sitting down to a nice Christmas dinner, my parents and I were headed into town to the hospital I was born in to get six stiches to close the wound. Some of my cousins still remember that day. In fact, Jim, who sent me a CD of the farmhouse demolition included a snapshot of that old boot scrapper, sitting all alone, still embraced by its concrete mounting base that used to be part of the door landing. Whenever I hear anyone say the word "shithead", I always think of that boot scrapper that caused me some pain on the front of my head on Christmas Day.

When the farm life became too difficult for Grandma King, she purchased a small house in the city. I helped my Dad & Uncles build an addition on the small house for her. Uncle Ervin became the sole occupant in the old farmhouse, except when I would come out and stay for weeks at a time during the summer. Although we didn't dine as well as when Grandma was there to do the cooking, we never went hungry. We may not have had as much homemade bread and pies as before, but Uncle Erv always had a good supply if ice cream in the old freezer.

Politics wasn't something I heard a lot about while growing up. I think it was the "kid" thing in me to tune out that kid of adult conversation, or I was outside playing ball with my neighborhood friends. From what discussions I did pick up on, most of the relation leaned towards democratic candidates. I was old enough to remember them talking about the election of Kennedy, and remember their sadness when he was assassinated. They were probably democratic leaning for all the right reasons then.

The slow methodical approach taken by the old Communist Party and reinforced by certain socialist leaning groups such as the Weather Underground, was slowly replacing the clean intensions of the Democratic Party. As with so many other Democrats, they never saw the transition happening, nor did they recognize its arrival and would probably deny that any takeover has taken place. But then again, that was the long range plan of the Communist Party. I guess they were successful in carrying out their log range plan just as the Japanese proved their planning ability in the automobile industry.

Chapter Ten

We Got School'd

As previously mentioned, my college days were almost uneventful in that there weren't as many outside activities to distract students as there are today. I lived the ordinary dormitory life as a freshman, capturing the same amount of mischief as anyone else. A few months before my freshman year, a friend and I had to attend a freshman orientation and also get signed up for classes. We had arrived at the college about three hours early so we could "check" things out. We drove into the city to the market square area where local vendors were selling the locally grown food items. My buddy & I each purchased a two pound bag of peas in a pod, and drove across the river and found a nice oak tree in a public park to sit under and eat our vegetables. I think we each ate our entire bags before driving back across the river to check out more of the city area. As we parked the car I felt the urge to go to the bathroom, but resisted as long as possible. After another twenty minute of walking around, the urge had turned to pain, and I had to find a bathroom... fast. As I darted towards the bathroom of an A&W root beer stand, my buddy announce the same need and yelled at me that he was headed across the street to a Clark gas station. About a half hour later we both simultaneously departed our respective dumping stations, and met on the corner. Both us looked like we had been run over by a truck. I think of that day every time I see peas in the pod in a store, or even if I see a pod in any selection of Chinese meals. I guess too much of a good thing at once is not a good decision.

The year I started college was the year that the legal drinking age in Wisconsin for liquor was lowered from 21 to 18. That was the largest distraction to freshmen starting their college life. Luckily, the cost of drinking as a freshman helped curb that activity. I'm fortunate that I didn't have a lot of extra spending money as I might have been tempted to exercise the new drinking age law more often. As it was, we visited a couple of entertainment bars within walking distance to the campus, The Pour House, and The Brat Barn, that sat across the road from one another and often featured some very good musical entertainment. Wisconsin is known for several things, one being the ample number of taverns or bars. Within a city block of the city's main market square area, there was something like 27 different drinking establishments. Some students (with a seemingly endless supply of money from their parents), went on weekend pub "crawls" which also described the way they returned to the college campus dorm area after a night on the town.

It was also in my freshmen year that I attended that Bill Ayers rally where I heard him denounce our need for our parents and family members. He kept repeating to not pay any attention to our parents and learn to think on our own. At one point he suggested that it would be better for most children if their parents were dead.

It was decades later that I realized that Goals 40 & 41 of the Communist Party platform were to: _**"Discredit the family as an institution. Encourage promiscuity and easy divorce"**_, and _**"Emphasize the need to raise children away from the negative influence of parents. Attribute prejudices, mental blocks and retarding to suppress influence of parents"**_. Is there any wonder why there is such a blatant disrespect for parents these days when that is what is encouraged in college these days? These go hand in hand with goals 17 & 18: _**"Get control of the schools. Use them as transmission belts for socialism and current propaganda. Soften the curriculum. Get control of the teacher's associations. Put the party line in textbooks"**_, and _**"Gain control of all student newspapers"**_. Is there a doubt why and how the teachers unions became entrenched with the left leaning government, now called the Democratic Party?

My second year of college I decided to leave the dormitory. I heard that the Boy Scouts were looking for a guardian at their summer camp during the off season, so I inquired about it at the local council office, and within a week heard back that my application had been accepted. My only duties were to show a presence there by inhabiting the 10 X 60 house trailer that they had there on site. The downside was that there was no running water at the camp or in the trailer during the winter months, so it was carrying water sourced from a local gas station and any bathroom needs would have to be satisfied by a one-holer out back. I showered regularly in the college locker room. I found a friend to share the trailer with, and we were able to do some car-pooling since our class schedules were similar.

During the snowy Wisconsin winter, various scout troops would reserve the camp for a winter outing. On the coldest Fridays of Wisconsin winters, I would walk up to the camp's main lodge and light a fire in the huge fire place in an attempt to start the warming process before the troops arrived. They always appreciated it, but in return, I would ask them to do some small tasks in return, like do some snow shoveling for me, or pull some snow off some of the roofs on buildings in camp. There was no vandalism that occurred during that year that I stayed at the Scout Camp and the camp was intact, when I turned the keys back over to the Council in May.

We survived, and no rent payments were a great help to my parents and my wallet, as we split the college expense 50/50.

In the past three or four years of this writing, I have talked to several sets of parents who have notice a great change coming out of college versus the way they went in. Most of these comments involve the same two colleges, one in Wisconsin, and one here in Kansas. Everyone said their kids were respectful to others, were involved in various church organizations, were thrifty with their money, and tolerated other people with different opinions, before they started college. They were just the opposite when they came out...anti-religion, anti-conservative, couldn't save a dime if their life depended on it, and would flip anyone off at the drop of a hat. Both schools are considered now to be very liberal in their views. Their school newspapers and website reek of anti-establishment stories, and socialistic views. When driving through the campus or nearby areas of either university, you can see a lot of Bill Ayers look-alikes, probably still wearing the same clothes that they wore in the 1960's. The Weather Underground that Bill Ayers was such a proud member of have carried out their "40 or 50-year plan with grace and diligence.

Now a day, there is a general consensus that only 21% of people polled believe that college grads have the proper skills to enter the workforce. Why? I believe there are way too many soft and bogus college majors available in today's colleges. Who ever heard of some of these soft majors thirty years ago? I believe there was an over-zealous attempt by the colleges and the government some twenty years ago to entice as many kids into college as possible, not for the good of the students, but for the selfish wants of the colleges. The high-paid liberal professors from the 60's need grandioso raises to keep them in their respective colleges, and the universities had to generate as much money as possible to keep them there. The subject of tenured professors is another beef I have. In reality, universities pay professors who have stayed on the job a larger salary to teach less. Yes, the more years a professor has under his belt, the more teaching assistants (TA's) he is allowed to have under his wing. The TA's end up teaching all the classes and the high paid professor can come in late and drink coffee. The tuition paying students get the penalty of a less experienced teacher and the college has to pay additional salaries for the part-time TA help. The students lose out, the universities lose out, and the phat and happy tenured professor gets a cakewalk while indoctrinating his helpers with his liberal stances.

In the past twenty years or so, there has also been a glut of money spent on athletic programs which were to bring in additional revenues to the colleges through increased enrollments and event ticket fees. But the costs of such programs and the coach's salaries made it virtually impossible for the schools to cover their expenses. State and federal dollars were at one time being manipulated to build lavish stadiums and practice facilities, instead of educational facilities, while other educational facilities were under-utilized.

The government shamed kids into going on to a higher education by saying their future depended on it. So, instead of a high school senior deciding to go to a trade school to become an electrician, builder, plumber or nurse, and make $20-$90 per hour, the kids of today are sitting at home after graduation without a job in their field of expertise trying to pay off a $40,000 - $100,000 loan, while shacking out on mom and dad's couch.

How about another victory for the Communist, now Democratic Party? How about their goals number 27 & 28? **_"Infiltrate the churches and replace revealed religion with "social" religion. Discredit the Bible and emphasize the need for intellectual maturity which does not need a "religious crutch"''_**, and, **_"Eliminate prayer or any phase of religious expression in the schools on the ground that it violates the principle of "separation of church and state."_** All this has happened and is still happening today, and all from what was planned out by the Communist party gurus before 1963.

You must have heard countless times of the removal of all prayer and religion from our public schools, in fear that it may intimidate or offend someone.
    "The removal of prayer from our schools was a violation of the third commandment which commands us "not to take the name of the Lord in vain." By the judicial act of forbidding invocation, the Court audaciously elevated a secularized

system of education beyond the authority, reach and blessing of God Himself. Worse than taking the Lord's sacred name in vain is treating it with contempt, denying it rightful place and stripping it from public use and even from the lips of children. Jesus' own expressed desire, "Let the little children come to Me, and do not forbid them" was also violated by these judges, many of whom were raised in Christian homes."[3]

Something else to consider; ……. their Communist Party Goal number 32: "***Support any socialist movement to give centralized control over any part of the culture – education, social agencies, welfare programs, mental health clinics, etc.***"

Anyone with any sight at all should have seen the change in our education system. If not, they just haven't been paying attention. Most of education social agencies and welfare programs are being directed by offices in Washington, DC, rather than by state or local authority. The "No Child Left Behind" program was actually twisted up to mean more like "Forget the Kids Who Can Excel". So much emphasis was placed on the poor student, that it took time away from challenging the good students to extend their goals.

In some parts of the country, the cost of education to the government is nearing $16,000 per year, per student, and the government thinks it needs to spend more. How about reigning in spending and evaluating what is the best educational bang for our "buck"? Large school system "campuses" are springing up all over the country, while the education outcome measured by standard testing is in decline. Now the government, with all its intelligence, is considering the lowering of test score requirements, so that their decisions and results look more favorable.

Taking a look at the current forms of art these days can be attributed to the communist party goals number 23: "***Control***

---

[3] ttp://www.forerunner.com/forerunner/X0098_Ban_on_school_prayer.html

art critics and directors of art museums. Our plan is to promote ugliness, repulsive, meaningless art." Young artist who create some of the modern trash in our current environments were students of this higher education and the new philosophies forced on them. And true, we are in an age that has output some new and pretty ugly artwork into our communities and schools, while our federal and local governments call it "The Art for the Ages".

Want to know why various groups launch protests on college campuses and government office doorsteps these days? They say they do it because of their freedom of speech, but the final result may just be the loss of that right. All we have to do is refer to number 42 of the communist goals of 1963: "*Create the impression that violence and insurrection are legitimate aspects on the American tradition; that students and special-interest groups should rise up to solve economic political or social problems*."

Why are there so many who want to change the United States constitution? Goals 29 & 30: "*Discredit the American constitution by calling it inadequate, old fashioned, all of step with modern needs, a hindrance to cooperation the nations on a worldwide basis,*" and "*Discredit the American founding fathers. Present them as selfish aristocrats would no concern for "common man.""*

If you have heard about schools illuminating a lot of U.S. history it's probably because the goal number 31 of the communist party: "*Belittle all forms of American culture and discourage the teaching of American history on the ground that it was only part of the "big picture." Give more emphasis to Russian history since the communists took over.*"

Grade schools and high schools are limiting the number of history hours required within their curriculum. Any history that is taught is beginning to look like the schools are dismissing some of our founding father information and important events in the creation of our country. Various school systems are contemplating dropping any history before 1877.[4] That's basically the first one hundred years of our county's existence. As soon as our early American history is no longer taught, we will have solidified our destination to that of a second world country.

I'm not sure about the feelings of anyone else but I'd say what we have witnessed over the past 10-15 years is a clear indication that the socialist, communist party has taken a stronghold within the United States of America and disguised themselves as members of the Democratic Party. The truth is evident. The truth is easy to see. If you look for proof on your own you will usually find it. But you have to want to see it with an open mind and heart. As Charles Payne wrote in a recent editorial, the current administration is showing us that "the whooping stick is replacing the olive branch."

---

[4] http://www.wcnc.com/news/local/Cut-Early-US-History-from-High-School-84158327.html

Chapter Eleven

Invasion for Political Reason

The mass exodus from Mexico to the United States in the past 20 years has sparked everyone's interest. They come here to find a better way of life for themselves, but do it in an improper manner. Now, our government is so lax in its border patrolling, people seem to be crossing at will. I bet we don't detain 1/5th of the number of people who are crossing. When they get here they fight our own citizens for the food on our tables. I don't mind fair competition, but when a company's bid for a highway construction job is based on his all legal citizen workforce versus a bid where undocumented workers are being utilized, the low bid will usually go to the lower labor cost bidder. And this happens every day, whether our government official tell us differently or not. I used to walk on construction sites with a camera during my working days and notice the workers scatter when I raised the camera up. One of our California reps used to say, "Watch this disappearing act." He would raise a camera to his eye as if to take a picture, and you could see at least 50% of the workers high tail it out of site. They would stay hidden until we would leave. Do you want to bet if they were illegals working on the construction crew?

Why are they allowed to come in so freely? Why did we send our jobs to Mexico, and are now offering to take in their unemployed?

Our government is lax in its border enforcement. We spend billions of dollars and sent twenty-thousand troops to help secure the border between North and South Korea, but are willing to only spend a fraction of that amount and manpower to police our own borders and safe-keep our own citizens.

President Clinton proudly signed a Free Trade Agreement with Mexico in the '90's, but it turned out to be a one-sided victory for the Mexicans. They are also eating our lunch, as we sent them our jobs and manufacturing and now we take in their unemployed, feed them, employ them, offer them free medical treatment, and conjure up a way to give them amnesty before allowing people from other countries to enter that have been standing in line for a long while. All of the above just invites more people to come across the border, and we might be only seeing the tip of the iceberg so far. Any amnesty program will bring a larger flood of people across the border.

Perhaps we should build an Army training center in the deserts of south Arizona. It would be a suitable place to train for our Middle East skirmishes and at the same time be able to guard our border with Mexico. We have bases all around the world to help protect those areas from invasions, but don't give a rip about our own borders.

In 2005, Cindy & I purchased a cruise package that departed from Seattle, heading for various ports in Alaska. We had a balcony room on the starboard side of the ship. We spent very little time there although the scenery was magnificent. We didn't want to spend too much time there, because we were afraid we were missing even better scenery on the port side of the ship, so we spent a lot of time standing on the scenic viewing area on the bow of the ship. Oddly, there weren't too many people there, because most had set their plans on enjoying some of the ships many other activities inside. Not us. We can visit a casino any day of the week at home or go to a movie theater any day of the week. Why do it on a ship in the midst of such great splendor and beauty. I can see where one might want to stay indoors if all you saw outside was a flat ocean. See it once, that's enough. But the Alaskan scenery shouldn't be discounted by anyone.

On the second to the last day of our scenic trip, the ship made a stop in Victoria, British Columbia, Canada. Everyone departing the ship had to show their USA passport to either get off the ship or get back on the ship. There were Canadian Customs personnel protecting their shores from illegal entrees, and there were ship officers checking passports for people re-boarding our ship before departure. But, we can't stop the masses of people entering our nation's southern borders. Why not? Because the powers to be aren't serious about sealing our borders off. Our leaders, in tune with the old Commie Party of yesteryear, want as many of the Mexican sympathetic prospective voters to climb across our borders as they can. Although our leaders claim that illegal entry is at its lowest level in years, there are still way too many coming over into our country every day. It is so easy, that other foreign entries like those from Al Qaeda, the Muslim Brotherhood, North Koreans, Iranians, etc., have an exceptionally easy path into destroying our country from within.

What about the people from other countries who want into our domain? Why are so many of them pushed to the back of the immigration entry list because of all the Mexicans cutting in line ahead of them? If we are supposed to be such a diverse nation, why the unequal amounts of nations being represented? Why do people from Argentina, Chile, Canada, Singapore, Australia, etc., have to wait on a list for years and years, because our immigration allowances are being consumed by illegal entry via the border with Mexico?

If you think for one second that the prices you pay at the grocery store are cheaper because of the low-waged illegal immigrants with six dependents making a paltry $5.00 per hour, you are very mistaken. When you consider that the illegal immigrant pays no taxes, but is able to receive Section 8 housing and subsidized rent, food stamps, free (no-deductible, no copay) healthcare insurance, free breakfast and lunch for his children at a school that now requires bi-lingual teachers at an added cost, energy bill relief, and at the end of the year he can file for Earned Income Credit" of up to $3,200 on a Federal Income Tax Return, PLUS, when he retires he can collect Social Security and Medicare even though he didn't pay in one dime to those funds. He is being paid his hourly rate of $5 per hour plus collects an additional $20.00 - $30.00 per hour as benefits for him and his family. This all is coming courtesy of us, the taxpayers.

Our governments Homeland Security department reports illegal border crossing to the President as in decline over the past couple of years, in fact the lowest in several years. But…… the rest of the story that is untold, it that in 2010, illegal border crossings have only been monitored and reported on only about 44% of the entire USA-Mexican border. Is this more gullibilitation? How many are crossing on the 56% of the borderline not being monitored or reported? I guess, if I were a person wanting to enter the USA, I would probably want to cross on part of the 56% not being monitored.

One reason is evident. The powers-to-be want some sympathetic votes out of the Mexican invaders, plain and simple. We are simply witnessing the out-of-control government our founding fathers warned us about. Sad, but this is very true.

Wake up America!

Chapter Twelve

Conspiracy?

Why did the Communists pick on the Democratic Party for take-over? Is it the truth that the Democratic Party movement leans towards enforcement by state control? State control, not meaning necessarily the individual states in the US, but it is the authoritarian approach as used by Communist nation administrators. They do this not always with the iron fist that everyone can see. They will softly try to convince everyone that their policies and regulations are for the good of the whole country either now or in the future. They will use convincing terms like, "our children's future", or "energy conservation awareness", or in "fairness to all", even when the opposite is their true intention. "Fair-Share" is the term of this administration, but in reality, what is being proposed is not "fair" at all. They tout "redistribution" as their mainstay objective, in other words, make the USA a nanny state. They claim they know what's best for everyone, even though you were never asked your opinion. During campaigns, you hear how delegates are so in touch with the people. Yeah, Riiiight. When the Presidential candidates visit a city their schedules are so rushed, they seldom take the chance to sit down with anyone. You see an occasional news clip of the presidential candidate visiting an ice cream shop or a small café, but it's for political advertising purposes, not for their own learning. They don't want to listen to the people. After all, what they would hear would probably be contrary to their agendas. And they love to twist the public opinion polls to look in their favor. They will ignore the fact that 65% of the people do not want a change to the second amendment, but will say they do by saying people do not want any more mass shootings......two different things, twisted into a favorable slant towards their agenda.

How many times do you hear a campaigner say, "I hear the voice of the people loud and clear"? They haven't heard anything more than their "Chief of Getting Re-elected Manager" tell them to say that, or they are reading a speech off a teleprompter, that someone has craftily designed to make them sound great and in-touch with their people.

I'm a simple man. Show me what you can do and I'll support you if I like what I am seeing. Feeding me bull crap and lying to me won't get my vote, and a lot of politicians are giving us a shovel full at the present time.

I suppose most people who always vote for the same party because their families have for decades never take the chance to smell the flowers around them. If they would stop to only look around a little bit, they might recognize what's happening and begin to investigate other paths. Politicians with ulterior motives are smart enough not to force anyone too heavy a dose of anything, but rather tend to piece-meal it out slowly so no one large chunk of anything is affected all at once.

Just because a teacher or professor said something in high school or college that caught your attention doesn't mean he was giving you a fair and balanced opinion. Too much of that unbalanced rhetoric is being shoveled out by left-leaning professors who either willingly or un-willingly are spreading anti-American sentiments, or possibly even Communistic ideals. Remember the Goals of 1963, number 17: "**_Get control of schools. Use them as transmission belt for socialism and Communist propaganda. Soften the curriculum. Get control of the teacher's associations._**"

Yup, they've been planning this for a long time. It is efficient and effective product planning by my estimation. They've cautiously and slowly fed us small doses of their magic elixir, and we never realized how sick we have become until it festers into an incurable disease.

Chapter Thirteen

Fighting the Battle

Almost five years after my diagnosis of having Inclusion Body Myositis, I am experiencing exactly what the experts and other IBM patients said would happen. I cannot stand from a seated position unless it is high enough to get my legs straight underneath me, lock my knees and shift my weight so I can balance over my feet. I can still "sort of" walk on a flat level surface, but outside the house, I can't walk ten feet on the lawn with something going wrong. Once I fall, it is impossible for me to get up. I have almost nothing left as far as muscles in my upper thighs, and my arms are useless because of no muscle left in my upper arms. My fingers have no gripping power any more, and I can't curl them up into a fist any more, unless I force them down with my other hand.

When I fall inside the house, my wife gets the 2' X 4' piece of old countertop that we mounted 2.5" casters underneath and added a rope on it. With the assistance of my wife, I get rolled up onto the wheeled platform and she pulls me to the master bathroom where I have a patient hoist system mounted. I use the hoist system to pick my 245 pound frame off the platform and to a standing position or into my powerchair.

I've taken some dandy spills during the past couple of years. So far, (knock on wood), I have not broken anything but my pride. My upper body has weakened so much that when I do fall, it is almost impossible to stop my head from hitting the floor hard. It seems that when I try to keep my head from hitting the floor, I can only momentarily hold it, and then a whiplash effect snaps my head into the floor without fail. I've survived many falls that created a good size "egg" bruise on my head. I would be a good lab rat for testing football helmets.

In 2006, my wife and I were returning from a trip to Vancouver, British Columbia where my son was playing a college basketball game. All went well during the trip until I stepped off the last step of the puddle-jumper airplane we had for the last leg of the trip. My leg buckled, and down I landed on the airport tarmac. In 2008, I walked up to the front of an elevator in a hotel lobby and stopped in front of the closed door. My knees seemed to keep going forward and I buckled and fell. I found a multi-tiered seat and plant stand to crawl up and get back into a standing position. Later during the night, I got out of the hotel bed and took a step towards the bathroom and my knees buckled again. This time I ground my bare knees into the hotel room carpet, and really skinned up my knees. I had to stay in the bathroom and painfully scrubbed my torn up knees to fight of any "yuck" from the hotel room carpet. Ouch! That trip was my last trip on an airplane. Since I cannot climb stairs or get up from a seated position, all my travel will be in my ramp van, where I am the co-pilot and my wife is the pilot.

I put a few bucks into making my house more accessible for the present and my future, but not as many dollars as one might think. If you go out and pay retail for everything, and then pay a carpenter or other specialist to do the labor, it can become quite costly. I try to keep one or two steps ahead of my dreadful disease's progression, and take time to shop for the best prices. I have found two patient lift systems, one that retailed for about $6,000, and the second one at about $4,500. I paid $1,800 for the first one and $475 for the second one. Both were in like new condition. My power chair regularly retails for about $24,000 and I found a like new one in Kansas City from a private party and paid $500. It had only 21 miles on the digital odometer, and looked brand new. Along with the powerchair came an extra $400 air-ride cushion. I paid $4,000 for the used elevator on Ebay, and a good friend donated his time to install it. It cost me probably another couple hundred dollars for other lumber and supplies to install it, and some beer, gin and vodka to wash down the dust after a long day's work.

We built a 20 foot long ramp for access to the front door. We recently installed a new fiberglass door with a special ADA threshold, and installed an automatic door opener at the same time at a combined cost of about $1,400. The automatic feature on the door allows me to go into and out of the house without the hassle of not being able to reach the door knob after driving my powerchair though the doorway. My ability to work on these projects has long left me, but I am still a good planner and straw boss. My wife, Cindy has jumped into many of these projects and did remarkable well. I kid her that she is now easy to buy gifts for....a new chainsaw, tile saw, lawn tractor, etc...., you know what I mean....! We got a lot of help from an old neighbor, Mike T., and also from my son and son-in-law.

My wife and I tackled a kitchen remodeling project last year (2011). I did all the planning & purchasing, and she did the demolition and with the help of the above plus Bob D., she completed the $30,000 kitchen makeover for about $13,000. It goes to prove that if you give a good woman a "saws-all", she can fix anything......

My wife had to quit her job in 2008 to stay at home and watch me and my IBM. She also started up a business a couple of years ago. I help her any way I can. We develop operators & parts manuals for small manufacturers who can't support a technical publication department of their own. We have been fortunate to have several clients that we do work for. We don't make a lot of money doing it, but it pays for some of the accessibility stuff we do, and it keeps our minds from straying into oblivion.

Now, I'm searching the on-line shopping sites for a hospital bed that will raise up high enough to help me get out of bed to go to the bathroom in the middle of the night without waking my wife. There are a lot of adjustable beds available from private parties, but few with a high-low capability. Purchasing a high-low bed will also allow me to more easily transfer from my powerchair to bed and vice-versa later, but for now will assist me to get to a standing position to keep me with some independence and pride. After I did a few searches on the internet for hi-low adjustable beds, it was evident that almost anyone can track what you are looking at on the internet. Without providing any information or requesting info from any supplier, I started to see ads pop up for adjustable beds by the companies that I had looked at and even more that I hadn't even looked at. One can say it helped me by showing me more prospective companies that offer the product I was looking for, but the other side of the coin is that your internet searches are being tracked and disseminated throughout the business world for almost anyone to have access to. If various companies can get access to what we are researching on the internet, you know that "Big Brother", our government, also has the capability of knowing what we are searching for. As I searched for copies of the Communist Party Goals of 1963 on the internet to reference for this book, am I now placed on the government's watch list...or will I suddenly start receiving invitations to donate money to the Democratic Party?

My residence has an ample amount of lawn to mow, and with my loss of strength, there will be a time in the near future that my wife will be doing the lawn work also. I recently purchased a nice riding lawnmower tractor to replace the zero-turn mower that I owned previously. She claimed she understood the operation of a standard tractor with a steering wheel much more than my zero-turn mower. I haven't completely given up on the lawn yet, but it is getting difficult to depress the left pedal that is required to start the engine. Oh well....

I have always taken pride in how my home and lawn look from the outside. I never neglect to mow my lawn like some people do. I fight the weeds as much as possible, more often than most people in our neighborhood. The days of the meticulous lawn care might be coming to an end, but as long as there is a will and a way, I'll try to keep it up.

As I make my preparations for the day when I will be bed-bound, i.e., eating, sleeping, watching TV and hopefully some computing, I hope that I will be practiced in the art of immobility by that time and have done everything possible to make it easy on my loving caregiver.

I am finding it hard to accept the fact that I am, indeed, on my last legs, literally.

Chapter Fourteen

Theft

This disease sucks! Not only is it robbing me from finishing a career and making money for my family, it is depriving me of a normal retirement. Since I already can't do a lot of things, I would certainly like to do a small amount of traveling before I am completely bedridden. That's not going to happen because we are babysitting for our daughter's son, our grandson every day. By the time he is school age, it will be most difficult to travel anywhere.

I spend my days wondering how the world is going to avail itself to the likes of my grandson when he turns into a young adult. Will he be able to direct his life the way he desires or the way our government desires? It's already become the norm that it's okay for the government to steal from us.

The current government thinks it is okay to wastefully spend our tax dollars and then ask for more. They grant their buddies on corporate boards millions of dollars in grants and loans that fill their pockets as a reward for supporting certain candidates. It's funny that the President's green energy buddies can fill their pockets with our taxpayer grant money without any taxes being paid on them, but we can't be later than Aril 15th with our tax payment or we get penalized.

The money granted or loaned to corporations is like a revolving door. The government gives Corporation "X" a set amount of our taxpayer money. Corporation X then takes some of that money and donates back to the political party that controls the piggybank, or as in some cases pay their corporate executives huge salary bonuses from the loaned amount. Although no one in a government office will admit it, but I'm convinced that the payback agreement was established before the initial loan was granted.

How controlling will our government be by 2025 if the current stream of socialist vampires gain more control of our money, personal property and personal rights? Will the United Nations be the controlling standard as stated in Communist Goal number 11: "***Promote the UN as the only hope for mankind, If its charter is rewritten, demand that it be set up as a one-world government with its own independent arm forces***." We saw a bit of that recently in 2012 when President Obama sided with the UN on a worldwide gun control ban proposal, meaning that our Second Amendment Rights would be cancelled by this world-wide legislation if enacted. Now the President is promoting the idea of letting the United Nations take over our drone program. If these types of things go through, it will be just a matter of time before our country will be a second or even a third rate country instead of being in the top tier as we are now.

What about President Obama's comment to the Russia's leaders unintentionally being caught on camera and microphone saying, "I will have more flexibility after the election." What's going to occur in his second term?

I am afraid, very afraid that my grandchildren's lives will be consumed by government (national or worldwide), and everyone might be just wards of the nation, or some kind of new world order. It might not be apparent to most, but it sure seems like the socialist party is slowly and methodically steering us in that direction. Once the takeover of the USA is on its way, it's just a matter of time until we are folded into the "world society", and many other countries will fall prey to the same if we collapse. It's identical to what my overseas friends said happened to them and are predicting the same for America.

The switch in the direction of healthcare being controlled by the government is already scary. We currently learn of some new aspect of government controlling our personal life choices every day. The Affordable Healthcare Act law has passed, but no one including many who wrote the law comprehends its entire contents or how it will be administered. Remembering the Japanese auto plan of years ago.......the older people will soon be gone and the next generation and their babies will have accepted Obamacare as the new status quo thus will not impede its operation. Any doubt if the enactment of Obamacare had anything to do with Goal number 32: "*__Support any socialist movement to give centralized control over any part of the culture—education, social agencies, welfare programs, mental health clinics, etc....__*"

My predictions drive me to think that there will be a drop in the level of medical care provided under the Affordable Care Act. Hospitals and clinics will not be able to afford the new technology equipment and afford payments on them at the so-called money-saving rates that the government will be willing to reimburse.

There is a huge bubble of baby boomers entering into retirement age. This bubble is causing havoc with the funding of Medicare. These baby boomers are living longer than originally anticipated and the average age at death for a USA citizen is now 77.8 years of age in 2007 according to the CDC.
[5]

Will the government allow the elderly to get high end healthcare or will they limit what they are eligible for, just to get them off the Medicare account? This is a gruesome question, but highly probable given that the Congress made sure "they" were not to be included in the same Affordable Care that the rest of us citizens will be place into.

What other rights are slowly dissolving into shades of gray and will soon disappear? One I can think of is the right of

---

[5] http://www.cdc.gov/nchs/data/nvsr/nvsr55/nvsr55_19.pdf

respect. This is not normally thought of as a right, but as an action of culture. Poor parental steering can probably be blamed for the lack of respect our young have for others today. Unfortunately, our current leaders want to strip the young out from the control of their parents at a younger age by offering free preschool to children.

Personal and material effects are being lost every day as acts of disrespect. Everyone is entitled to their opinion no matter what it is, but lately, even those voicing their opinion along with acts of violence are not subject to the old standard laws of the land. If a bunch of students gather for a protest and it gets out of hand, many times they "might' receive a slap on the wrist before being released under some presumed "right to assemble" regulation. But again, the student uprisings have gained popularity partly caused by the 1963 goal number 19: "***Use student riots to foment public protests against programs or organizations which are under Communist attack***." Occupy Wall Street and the actions of students on Oakland, CA in 2011-12 come to mind. The student protests spread like wild-fire among other unemployed bodies, and neighbors and businesses in those areas had to endure months of agony and loss of liberties and freedoms. Why weren't the police more active in resolving the problem rather than the abrogation by the city officials? Didn't the residents in those affected areas have more rights to their possessions than the uprising masses did? If I pay public taxes on a building that supports my livelihood, I would expect the law to make sure that my business was available to customers, and not be blocked by a bunch of rabble-rousers.

Some more rabble-rousing is being protected by current law enforcement involves the lack of respect to our cultural standards of morality. All you have to do is turn on the TV set to see how promiscuous the shows are becoming or have become. Watching a show the other night, the bad-language "beep" occurred more than 100 times during a 30 minute show. But the words off the lips of the actors could be read by any fifth grader. The F-bomb was bleeped no less than 50 times, I swear, but the lip motions were easily detectable, so what the hell...why bleep it out? Everyone knows what was said. Perhaps all this degenerate speech these days reverts back to Goal number 25: *"**Break down cultural standards of morality by promoting pornography and obscenity in books, magazines, motion pictures, radio and TV**"*. Also number 24: *"**Eliminate all laws governing obscenity by calling them "censorship" and a violation of free speech and free press.**"* Is there any doubt where all these actions originated?

Most Democrats in Congress would vote for a ban on all guns if they didn't have to face their voters every four years. The second amendment reads, "A well regulated militia being necessary to the security of a free state, the right of the people to keep and bear arms shall not be infringed." [6]

It was not until 2008 that the Supreme Court definitively came down on the side of an "individual rights" theory. Relyingon new scholarship regarding the origins of the Amendment, the Court in District of Columbia v. Heller confirmed what had been a growing consensus of legal scholars – that the rights of the Second Amendment adhered to individuals. The Court reached this conclusion after a textual analysis of the Amendment, an examination of the historical use of prefatory phrases in statutes, and a detailed exploration of the 18th century meaning of phrases found in the Amendment. Although accepting that the historical and contemporaneous use of the phrase "keep and bear Arms" often arose in connection with military activities, the Court noted that its use was not limited to those contexts. Further, the Court found that the phrase "well-regulated Militia" referred not to formally organized state or federal militias, but to the pool of "able-bodied men" who were

---

[6]   http://www.gpo.gov/fdsys/pkg/GPO-CONAN-2008/pdf/GPO-CONAN-2008.pdf

available for conscription. Finally, the Court reviewed contemporaneous state constitutions, post-enactment commentary and subsequent case law to conclude that the purpose of the right to keep and bear arms extended beyond the context of militia service to include self-defense. [7]

Although the above court decision is front and center, the progressive left is attempting to gain public support for banning guns by capitalizing on the mass shootings in Colorado and Connecticut. These "lefties" seem to have taken a liking to taking advantage of every "catastrophe."

Raum Emanuel, former advisor to President Obama and now Mayor of Chicago often said, "Never let a crisis go to waste." I guess this could be why we hear so much blame being thrown around these days, and promises for improvement that never materialize.

---

[7]   http://www.gpo.gov/fdsys/pkg/GPO-CONAN-2008/pdf/GPO-CONAN-2008.pdf (page 82)

Chapter Fifteen

History

It doesn't take much investigative work to realize why Rome collapsed, and why countries like France, Japan and others have struggled so much in comparison to the United States and England.

In all these cases, either inflation or excessive spending or resource misappropriation of funds caused the demise or chances of recovery in rough times. In each case, the government depleted the resources available, and attempted to empty the pocketbooks of their citizens in an attempt to keep their regimes afloat.

The same is happening here in the USA. Due to a gross mishandling of our tax dollars where our government leaders thought it was most important to study the sexual habits of the Brazilian ant, we have now run short of money coming into the national coffers, and have amassed an almost $17 trillion in debt, with little chance for recovery. We never faced a major war in the last fifty years, or experienced a nuclear holocaust, or even a broad spread shortage of food. If American citizens had a good reason to protest, like for a shortage of food or water, that would be one thing, but when you see violent demonstrations wrecking your local Best Buy store rather than ransacking a food store, it is a sign that people are discontent about things other than life-sustaining items, as were the cases in Rome, Japan, France and others collapses.

Perhaps the masses should be converging on some of the big businesses that took their product manufacturing overseas and stole American jobs from our own people. Perhaps we should be protesting at the gates of George Bush or Bill Clinton's homes for signing those Free Trade Agreements in the 90's. Why couldn't people see this disaster coming?

Instead, let's sign into the "world globalization" as called for by socialist administrators and get this whole world on an even keel! Yeah,...Riiiight! In the swoop of a President's pen, America agreed to prop up other countries at the expense of our own. Our big businesses bought into the globalization plan hook, line and sinker, and promoted it as a way to increase their profits by utilizing cheaper labor in other parts of the world. Am I alone in thinking that in thinking it is abnormal for a huge company like GE to ship good paying jobs overseas, amass enormous profits, and additionally not pay any federal taxes on those profits?

And all this garbage about redistribution is nothing but a bunch of socialist rhetoric. History has shown that a government's redistribution of wealth can prove more destructive than even the most deadly enemy. Other countries have tried it and failed. Why would it work for us? Why should anyone agree that by making the rich poorer, the poorer would somehow be made richer? I haven't been employed by to many employers, but I have never been hired by a poor person yet! And the fair-share language of our current administration is sickening. They want hard-working people to be the soul (and soul) supporters of those that don't want to work or refuse to work because of all the good bennies they get from our government. The cost of these entitlements is astronomical, and all come from the working man's pockets.

Tea partiers tried to raise the level of awareness in the US a couple of years ago. They were shot down by the same liberal midgets that collect the freebies from the government. I don't think the Tea Party is as dead as most think it is, and their voice will continue to be heard in coming years. The original Tea Party originated as a result of unfair taxation. The current Tea Party is based on unfair taxation and the deliberate wasting of the taxpayer's dime.

Have Americans given up? Have they already folded between the goalposts of the socialists? It almost seems like it. One can hardly believe all that has happened in the last twenty years. From the degrading of our education system, to the government's takeover of the healthcare system, it's more than just normal that all has headed in the direction pointed out in 1963 in the Communist Party Goals. It is long since they have been called that, but I think it is evident that they intentionally traded their name for the one that used to be our Democratic Party. It doesn't seem to make a difference anymore if you are a Democrat or a Republican, the fact is do you want to be a Communist or an American. The Republican plan is 200+ years old here in the USA; while the Democrat's new party is less than 30 years old. From what I've read in history books versus what I am seeing taking place in recent society, I would take the side of using the old conservative anytime.

Chapter Sixteen

Our Environs

I will be the first one to admit that I do not want to see any flagrant harm done to our precious environment. I've spent a lot of time in the outdoors; on our nation's lakes, in our nation's forests, on our nation's highways, parks, cities and country sides. I have never agreed the idea of littering as I see a lot of people do today. I guess it gets back to that "respect" topic I spoke of a few chapters back. If you can't exhibit respect for other people, why would I believe you would be kind to our environment? If I see you litter along our highways or on our lakes, wouldn't it be conceivable to believe you probably do that with other aspects of your life also?

Having said that........I am getting more and more pessimistic of the goodie-too-shoes approach that most of our environmental groups have become. Fact in point......In the State of Hawaii, a resident must request permission to cut down any native tree on their own property. In most cases, it is almost impossible for it to happen. They don't want to disturb the Hawaiian pristine environment. I guess I can go along with that. But in the same notion, I read that our government is forwarding about five billion dollars to construct a 20 mile long rail system through the middle of Oahu, to help curb some of the traffic issues there. I can possibly be convinced it may be a good idea. BUT....where are all the environmental geeks who won't let anyone else touch a native tree when it comes to this 20 mile project through Hawaii's largest island? We would probably be wrong if we assumed there weren't any native trees that will get bulldozed for that government supported project. When are the double standards going to end? Why is it okay for the government to steal from our environment, but it is illegal for the citizen to steal from the environment? The government touts improvement, but the citizen is accused of a crime.

Chapter Seventeen

Waking Up is hard to do

When you have what doctors say is a disease for which there are no medicines to combat it, there are times when you wake up a little depressed with the anxieties that accompany that fact. There are other days that you wake up with a fresh attitude, ready for what life is preparing to hand you. And some days, you wake up after a seldom good night's sleep, turn on the news or pick up the local newspaper and that good day is spoiled.

Today was just one of those days!

I just read in our local rag how our president is flying around the United States in our taxpayer paid jumbo jet (that costs about $200,000 an hour to operate) promoting free preschool for all of America. Now, I'm not one for holding back the educational start of our young citizens, if I believed that was all he was up to. But since my experiences and investigative outlook on life makes me believe there's an alternative motive to almost everything our leftist President does these days, I'll turn back to our favorite list of goals of 1963, Item 41 says, "***Emphasize the need to raise children away from the negative influence of parents. Attribute prejudices, mental blocks and retarding of children to suppressive influence of parents.***" These are not my words, but theirs! As far back as Marx and Engels, the communists argued for the dissolution of the family and the introduction of communal child-rearing. They want to start brainwashing our children at a younger age.

Additionally, in a recent major study by the U.S. Department of Health and Human Services, Head Start, the often touted programs revered by the left, revealed that children who were in the Head Start Programs generally do worse in math and have more problems with social interaction by the time that child reaches the third grade, compared to children from the same neighborhood who were not in the program. Therefore the benefits from this $8 billion program are negligible. So why should we as taxpayers agree to the government spending even one more dime on this type of program, if their own Department of HHS reports its failure? Perhaps this would be a good way to save some taxpayers some money over the next 10 years.

Are the caring words spoken by our president from his heart on our behalf or his behalf? Or is this being done as a result of his training by a multitude of professed American Communist Party advocates that he clung onto for years, almost since his birth. In my humble opinion, he should spend more time promoting more positive family principles and spend no time on ripping babies away from their parent's arms.

Perhaps I was raised by a loving mother who didn't believe in getting a job until after us kids were in school full-time. Perhaps I was lucky to have a wife that stayed at home to nurture our two children in their younger years. And what worked for us may not be good for everyone else. I can appreciate the necessity for some families to have two incomes to support their family, but I can't understand the alarming number of single parent families now in the USA. It's alarming to think that over 41% of births in the USA were to unwed mothers in 2011. [8] That number was 18.4% in 1980.[9]

I am not trying to open up a can of racial talk here, but of the above mentioned number, 71% of black babies born in the USA these days are as a result of an unwed mother situation, 66% of all native Indians, and 53% of all babies born in a Hispanic setting. Even the 29% for white women and 17% for

---

[8] http://www.singleparentsuccess.org/stats.html
[9] http://educationviews.org/skyrocketing-single-parent-births-could-signal-more-problems-for-education/

Asian women is alarming. 99% of all teens under the age of fifteen having babies are unwed.[10]

And what about the mothers who participate in illegal drugs purchased off the streets of our country?

"Alcohol and drug-addicted parents are more often involved in divorce, unemployment, domestic violence and legal problems, severely affecting their ability to be effective parents. A higher incidence of eating disorders, depression, anxiety and attempts at suicide exist among their children than in the general population. Physical and sexual abuse is more likely to happen in families where there is abuse of alcohol or drugs. Children from these homes are likely to have lower self-esteem and perceive themselves as unable to have control over their circumstances. Because of their stressors at home, children of substance abusers are more likely to experience problems in school, ranging from learning disabilities and failing grades to truancy and being expelled from school, notes the Center on Addiction and the Family." [11]

Is the problem in our society one that stems from the lack of mandatory preschool, or is it because of the lack of responsibility when it comes to sex and child-bearing? Or is it simply part of the Socialist goal of 1963, item 40: ***"Discredit the family as an institution. Encourage promiscuity and easy divorce."***

It's sad to go to sleep thinking about these things, and it's sad to wake up to news that our government is further playing into the hands of the Socialist demons that ruined other countries as well. The other countries were easy compared to the USA that for so many years stood firm with the guidance of the Constitution and Amendments.

---

[10] http://www.childtrendsdatabank.org/?q=node/196
[11] http://www.livestrong.com/article/495234-the-effects-of-drug-addicted-parents-on-children/

Now, this evil force is among us, dividing and conquering our bodies and souls, just as Myositis is overtaking me, slowly but progressively. Contrary to the specialists in the world that find it difficult to find a cure for my disease, our government is doing nothing to curtail our child development problems stemming from inadequate home lives.

Perhaps there should be a demerit program for parents. If you get pregnant before you are 18, you get 1 demerit. If you get pregnant out of wedlock, you get one more demerit. If you are a drug user (checked by blood test), you earn another demerit. If you get a divorce, you earn another demerit. If you don't keep up on your child support payments, you get another demerit. If you get a divorce with children in your responsibility, you get another demerit, If you are involved in any crime while carrying a rifle, shotgun, handgun of any kind, you get a demerit, etc., etc., etc. If you accumulate any combination of two demerits, you are not eligible for government assistance of "any" kind. Perhaps a program of this magnitude would get people to think a little bit before taking irresponsible actions.

Now a day, the law profession has made divorce an easy thing. Billboards advertising $495 divorces adorn our highways, streets and Yellow Pages. Lawyers can "specialize " in divorce cases only just like a doctor can specialize in heart or lung disease. The promise for "respectful dissolution of marriage" at bargain bin costs, make it easy for any couple to turn direction rather than "making it work." Too many divorces stem from money problems, or just the desire to "trade up" to something better or different. Marriage is now considered by some to be similar to a purchase of a car, in that once you get tired of one, you get rid of the one you have and get different one. The Socialist Party, now known as the Democrats must love this. That's another one of the Goals of '63 they can cross off as completed or at least moving in their intended direction. And where did this change occur? The easy divorce methods came directly out of liberal think tank colleges, littered with liberal and socialist professors, already in place to help their socialist cause.

Every year, the populations of liberal minded lawyers grow because of the plantation of ultra-liberal mindset professors employed in our law schools. When there is a glut of lawyers, more and more of them will utilize their entrepreneurial wit to promote different ways to make their practices thrive. Some of those actions involve the swaying of our personal rights. It seems that if a hard working person with money looks sideways at someone who doesn't give a rat's "arse" about anything, there will be a lawyer to offer a law suit against the richer of the two. There are plenty of ambulance chasers as exhibited on local TV ads. All present the promise of wealth to the people presumed as the unfortunate. I label some of them as unfortunate, because they sometimes may cause their own injury by actions that are deemed irresponsible or even stupid, but hope to claim a lawsuit against the non-guilty party. The "no-pay, if you don't win" gimmick that attorneys advertise invite all kinds of frivolous lawsuits.

Waking up is sometimes a hard thing to do, but you must learn to work through it.

Chapter Eighteen

Stupid

Did you ever do something that really seemed silly and can't believe you did that? It's happened to me already, and is possible starting to become more regular as I age. I guess it's just an aging thing.

But what really bothers me is when young educated people do things not out of error but out of stupidity or ignorance. I went to a high school baseball game a few years back and went to the concession stand to purchase some treats..., a $1.50 can of soda pop and a $.75 bag of sunflower seeds. I gave the young gal, who I later learned was a senior, three one dollar bills. She leaned down below the counter and pulled out a calculator. First she added the $1.50 item and the $.75 cent item, and came up with her total. She then counted out my three $1 bills, entered three, point, zero, zero, into her calculator and then subtracted her previously determined total of good purchased to come up with the change she needed to return to me. All of this while a line of people stood behind me waiting for their time to again witness this phenomenon. Later in the game, I went back for another can of soda pop, and handed a different girl two one-dollar bills. This girl didn't require a calculator so I partially regained my feelings towards the education system of today. As I turned around and started to open my soda, I looked at the change she gave me and noticed that she had given me two Susan B. Anthony dollar coins instead of two quarters. That again wiped out my good feelings about today's kids in today's education system.

I walked up to a large retail store checkout counter at local Kohl's department store just as the computers went down. My check out girl still had her drawer open, and the checkout supervisor told her to keep her drawer open so she could take care of anyone who wanted to pay with cash. The supervisor pulled a calculator out of her drawer and asked the cashier if she could add up my purchases and apply the sales tax. She said she could probably do it if she knew what the sales tax was. Her supervisor told her 7.3%, so the checkout gal entered my purchase of $29.95 and added $7.30 onto it. I knew there was an error when she looked at me and asked for $37.25 instead of just over $32 that I roughly calculated in my head. She insisted she did her calculating the way she was told, so I beckoned the supervisor over to remedy the situation. Our kids are entering the job market and don't know math basics. How sad I feel for the school systems, and how sad I feel for America.

But then again, it's what some of our leaders want. They want to grow kids not to be independent, but to be dependent on someone or something else. I don't blame the individual teachers, I blame the leaders who direct what the curriculum will be and how it is tested and measured. I blame the school administrators for not firing the bad or ineffective teachers. I blame the parent of the kids who do not take interest in how their child is doing in school and neglect to work with the child to help him improve.

Have you heard that some of the major textbook manufacturers and suppliers being pressured by leftist liberals to take a lot of American history out of our children's text books? It will be only a few years down the road when our children will learn absolutely nothing about our founding fathers if this goes through. Why? If you can predict what I am about to say, you haven't been paying attention. The socialists want to take control of the schools. In that fight, they want to discredit our founding father's rolls in the establishment of this unique country in an attempt to make it like so many others.

Chapter Nineteen

More Stupid

Every year The Myositis Association (TMA) hosts a national conference somewhere in the USA. Two years ago, it was in Las Vegas. My wife and I attended that conference. Last year it was held in Orlando, and in October of 2013, it is scheduled for Louisville, KY. As we did not want to land in the same situation where our handicap equipped room was a 0.6 mile from the conference rooms as we did in Las Vegas, I called the designated conference hotel in Louisville in early February to make sure I got a handicap room close to the action.

I called the hotel number as instructed by the TMA, and asked for "reservations" when the hotel answered the phone. After being transferred, I talked to a young man who seemed eager to arrange my stay, but could not find any instructions about booking a room for the TMA conference. I explained to him and even spelled out the word M-Y-O-S-I-T-I-S for him and explained that other members had already stated on the TMA blog that they had already made reservations. He said he would transfer me to the hotel's group reservation department. After a few moments, someone answered the phone, identified herself and asked me, "Where do you want to go?" I paused a bit, and established with her that I wanted to stay at her hotel in Louisville. She told me there were two hotels in Louisville that she could book me at. I told her I wanted the location that I originally called and gave her the number.

During this whole episode, my wife seated next to me in my home office is laughing her "you-know-what" off. I further explained that I called the hotel to make a reservation and their reservation group transferred me to this number. She told me I had been transferred to the hotel chain's national reservation desk but that she could possible take care of me.

I explained that I required an accessible room with a roll-in shower. After a quite a lengthy discussion, she said she would note a request on my reservation and hopefully the hotel could honor that request. When I told her that our trip depended on being guaranteed an accessible room preferably with two beds, she said she would transfer me to another number. I was transferred to a third number, they picked up and asked if I could hold, and immediately placed me in contact with some of the most loud and obnoxious music I have ever heard on the phone while on hold. You know...... the type that is so loud that it strains the speakers on your cell phone.

After a five minute wait, and so far 23 minutes tied up since I first dialed the phone, I hung up and redialed the original hotel number in Louisville. Again asking for the reservation group, I got a different person than I originally spoke with and spent the next five minutes explaining the rigmarole that I just encountered since first calling now 29 minutes ago. She was very apologetic and stated that she would try to help me and stated that she would not be transferring me to anyone else. But......, after about ten more minutes of her trying to find our TMA group in their computer system, she said she had placed us in their reservation system for a four night stay as requested and asked for my credit card number. After getting that info from me, she said she had reserved a King Bed handicap room with a roll-in shower. I said, "No", I had asked for a handicap room with a roll-in shower and two beds. She said she would make a note on the reservation requesting two beds, but could not promise anything. I again told her that my trip depended on being guaranteed that kind of room.

By this time, my wife was no longer laughing and was making side comments that she no longer wanted to make this conference trip. After being placed on hold for another undetermined amount of time, the phone went 'click" and the phone when silent.....no loud music, no dial tone, no person ...nothing. I hung up the phone and called the TMA national headquarters to report the 45 minute incident, and while on the phone explaining my experience with their selected hotel in Louisville, I received an email confirmation with the type of room I requested...guaranteed! Whoops...they have me down for only one person in the room when I explicitly told her, "two people....my wife and I". With all the national and international travel that I did during my career, this was the most aggravating and longest fight to reserve a hotel room....eight months in advance! Years ago, hotel reservations were filled out by hand and placed in a card catalog box.

Unfortunately, some people on the north end of a south bound computer are proving not as efficient, as exampled in this incident!

Chapter Twenty

IBM

If I tell people I have IBM, they think I'm going to tell them a computer joke. But Inclusion Body Myositis is unfortunately not a joke. It's serious stuff. The body's large muscles closest to the main trunk and the small muscles furthest away from the main trunk are affected. The main loss of pushing anything with leg or arm muscles is permanently lost in a slow progressive manner. During the progression of this disease, I found it more and more difficult to stand from a seated position. I purchased a lift chair recliner just to be able to get up from a chair in our living room. Now, that lift chair is getting difficult to get out of. Because I have no push power, I cannot climb even the smallest of stairs, and always have to depend on a ramp to ascend or descend any raised locations. When I fall, I do not have the push power left in my arms to push my upper body up to a sitting position. I can still slowly walk on a hard flat surface, but make me walk across a grass or soft surface, and I'll be on the ground in no time. It's the pits. Sometimes people drive past my house and see me getting off my power chair or scooter in the garage or I'll be getting on my riding lawn tractor. The next time they see me, I'll be riding my power chair 150 feet down our street to the mailbox. I bet they ask each other how I can walk in the garage, but not out on the street to the mailbox. I would answer that by inviting them to walk in my IBM shoes any day.

Inclusion-body myositis (IBM) is found in more men than women with onset usually occurring after age 50. A small number of IBM cases may be hereditary (h-IBM) but most are "sporadic" (s-IBM) meaning there is not a direct genetic link. In most cases, IBM progresses slowly over months or years. There is currently no effective treatment for IBM, although current gene therapy trials supported by TMA show promise.[12]

I fit that text book definition. I was about 53 when I noticed a loss of grasping strength in my right hand. Eight years later this disease has me in my power chair 90 percent of the time, with no ability to climb stairs, get up from a seated position or pull anything because of such weakness in my fingertips. I pray that I have the sporadic type, as I don't want any of my family members to find out someday that they carry the same disease.

My computer typing skills were never polished as they should have been. The only typing that I ever learned was with my two forefingers. In high school typing class, I could keep up with the best of typists until the teacher would stand next to me and place a piece of paper between my eyes and keyboard. Perhaps it was only practice for now when my fingers no longer flex or bend, and I have to use my stiff fingers to type this book.....that and a little help sometimes from the Microsoft speech recognition program on my computer. Yes, this entire book was typed with single finger strokes and sometimes by talking into a microphone and let the computer do the manual work.

When using the voice recognition program, it pays to stay healthy and not have a head cold. At about page thirty, I came down with a head cold that changed my voice for a few days, and I had to rely solely on the single finger plunking on the keyboard, and have used the single finger typing mode almost exclusively since. Now I can no longer use my forefinger on my left hand and have to use my middle finger. My biggest problem is hitting more than one key at a time, causing a lot of corrections. I'm sure I'm not the first person

---

[12] http://www.myositis.org/learn-about-myositis/types-of-myositis/inclusion-body-myositis

without normal typing skills to write a book, but I might be one of the first with IBM to write one!

I volunteered to form and be a group leader for a local Myositis Support Group. TMA has groups called KIT groups across the USA. KIT stands for Keep In Touch. For the past three years I belonged to a KIT group in Kansas City. Because the 6 hour round trip was a bit long for me, and the price of gasoline made it an expensive day outing for a two hour meeting, I decided to start a group here in the Wichita area. I contacted the TMA national office and they sent out a letter of invitation for us having our first meeting in January 2013. In seeing that there were a number of Myositis folks in Southern Kansas and no KIT group in all of Oklahoma, invitations were sent out as far away from Wichita as Norman, Oklahoma. Although it was a bit of a drive, we had a couple from the north side of Oklahoma City attend our first meeting, about a three hour drive each way. We hope the word of our support group spreads and we can build on the 15 people that attended our first meeting.

Myositis is one of those rare diseases that plead for more attention from the medical society. From time to time, there are only a few clinical tests going on at one time, but advances towards learning what the cause may be or what a cure might consist of, are still a long ways off. I have resolved that any cure found in the future might be of use for future generations, but a cure at this time will not bring back the muscles that have been lost. Very few doctors can identify with knowing anything about myositis, and even fewer have any notion about inclusion body myositis.

When my muscles are in the active degeneration mode in my case, as I call it, they feel like there are a million ants crawling around underneath my skin. Other times it is like someone pouring some gas on some Styrofoam inside my legs, and something was dissolving. There was some pain encountered during these times, but the pain was bearable, but the question about what was happening was mentally excruciating. At one point, the pain was so noticed in my left forearm, that I thought I might had broken a bone during a fall and went to my family doctor for an x-ray. Negative results were read, and I went home with the pain.

Every time I fall, a large chunk of pride and self-dignity goes away. My falls usually occur when one of my feet do not lift high enough off the floor surface and the front of my shoe catches the rock hard wood floor. My knee buckles and down I go. Not a pretty sight and usually seems to happen in slow motion.

My wife and I have become friends with a couple who reside north of Wichita. She, Carolyn, also has IBM. Her muscle degeneration is a bit behind me, as she still works two days a week as a surgical nurse. Her approach to soothing some of the discomfort is going to visit an acupuncturist every two weeks. She has asked her acupuncturist to come speak to our Myositis KIT during our next planned meeting in May. Her husband is a retired reverend at one of the local churches. Good folks, great new friends....... She co-leads the Myositis KIT Group with me.

Diagnosing Inclusion Body Myositis[13]

Blood Tests

There are a number of blood tests the doctor may choose. The following is a list of some of these. Unless otherwise noted, all of these tests require taking a sample of blood by using a needle. Only a small amount of discomfort and bruising should occur.

---

[13] http://www.myositis.org/learn-about-myositis

Aldolase Test

Aldolase is a substance found especially in the muscles. When muscles are damaged, the muscle cells break open and spill their contents (including aldolase) into the blood. Therefore, the amount of aldolase in the blood shows the extent of muscle damage. As the muscle damage becomes worse, the amount of aldolase in the muscle decreases over time.

 Since muscle weakness can be due to a neurological or a muscular problem, this test finds which is causing the weakness. Aldolase will not change when weakness is caused by neurological problems.

Antinuclear Antibodies Test (Also known as ANA Test)

Antibodies are an important part of our immune system. They fight infections, viruses and other "invaders." Antinuclear antibodies (ANA) are found in the blood of those patients whose immune systems are more likely to fight their bodies' own tissues, or those with autoimmune diseases.

Creatine Phosphokinase Test (Also known as CPK, Creatine Kinase, or CK Test)

 CPK, also known as creatine kinase, or CK, is a type of protein called an enzyme. It helps a reaction to occur. The normal function of CPK in our cells is to turn creatine into phosphate, which is burned as a quick source of energy by our cells.

When muscle is damaged, muscle cells break open and spill their contents into the bloodstream. Because most of the CPK in the body normally exists in muscle, a rise in the amount of CPK in the blood indicates that muscle damage has occurred, or is occurring. The type of CPK found in the blood determines what has been damaged (i.e. heart, brain, muscle).

CPK tests are used to evaluate suspected myositis when other symptoms are not present, to tell whether you have myositis or another neuromuscular disorder, or to check the progress of the disease after treatment.

For this test, a blood sample is taken, a procedure that may be repeated over a period of time for more accurate results. For this reason, if you're scheduled to have blood drawn for a CPK test, you should limit your exercise to normal activities before the test. Certain medicines may also affect the results of the test, so be sure to check with your doctor if you are taking any type of medications at all, including aspirin.

In a healthy adult, the CPK level in the blood serum varies with a number of factors (gender, race and activity), but normal range is 22 to 198 U/L (units per liter). Higher amounts of serum CPK can indicate muscle damage from chronic disease or acute muscle injury.

If the CPK test indicates muscle damage, more tests will be needed to find exactly where the muscle damage occurred.

Myositis patients often question why they may feel better or worse than their CPK levels indicate. The reason for that is the levels may lag behind the improvement or worsening of the disease.

Sed Rate (Also called ESR, or erythrocyte sedimentation rate) The Sed rate, or erythrocyte sedimentation rate, is another method for measuring swelling and inflammation of the muscles. Doctors use the Sed rate to watch the progress of the muscle inflammation. This test is not specific to a particular disease but to the presence of the inflammation.

For this test, the technicians mix red blood cells from the blood sample in a prepared test tube. They measure the length of time it takes these cells to settle to the bottom of the tube. For males, the normal rate falls between 0 and 15 millimeters per hour; females, 0 to 20 millimeters per hour. The Sed rate will be higher with more inflammation. (The Sed rate might be slightly higher if you are older or if pregnant.)

Other Blood Tests

Alanine aminotransferase (ALT, also called serum glutamate pyruvate transaminase [SGPT]) is an enzyme found in many tissues, including muscle. Normal ranges vary by age, gender, and other factors.

Aspartate aminotransferase (AST, also called serum glutamic-oxaloacetic transaminase [SGOT]) is a protein found in muscle and liver tissue.

Factor VIII-related antigen (also called von Willebrand factor VIII-related antigen) shows damage to the lining of the blood vessels and helps doctors check the level of the problem, especially in juvenile myositis (JM), to decide the right treatment plan.

Flow cytometry looks at a specific group of white blood cells and is used to learn more about the extent and severity of juvenile myositis (JM).

Lactate dehydrogenase is an enzyme found in skeletal muscle tissue. Normal values vary, but typical values range from 105 to 333 IU/L (international units per liter).

Muscle biopsy

Depending on the results of other lab tests, your doctor may order a muscle biopsy. The biopsy is one of the best ways to diagnose myositis and other muscle disorders. For this test, a doctor will remove a piece of your muscle tissue and study it under a microscope for abnormalities.

How is a muscle biopsy done?

A muscle biopsy can usually be done under local anesthesia (numbness to a specific area). A needle biopsy may be used for children and for adults with chronic conditions. The doctor puts a needle into your muscle and removes a small piece of tissue. Watch a video of a needle biopsy.

Other times an open biopsy is needed, where a wider area is sampled. This is the same test but requires cutting the skin to get to the muscle tissue.

Your doctor will choose the muscle depending on where you are feeling the pain and weakness. Most likely, he or she will avoid muscles already tested by a recent EMG or muscle biopsy. MRI's are now widely used to locate affected muscles to biopsy.

Will it hurt?
There is usually little or no pain with this test but instead an uncomfortable tugging feeling. However, some people report more pain depending on the size of the muscle sample taken. If you have an open biopsy, you may feel more pain than with a needle biopsy because of the amount of muscle tissue removed.

What are the risks of having this test?

There are few risks with this test. Any time your skin is broken, there is a small risk of infection at that spot. There also may be some bleeding or bruising.

What do the results of this test mean?
If the doctor sees something unusual about the muscle that was tested, he or she will run as many tests on that muscle as necessary to decide what type of muscle condition you may have. The results can show conditions such as inflammation, or swelling, of the muscle; damage to the muscle; and loss of muscle mass, or atrophy.

Electromyogram or EMG
An electromyogram, or EMG, is a test that measures the activity of the muscles. The test gathers information about the muscular and nervous systems.

An EMG is a way of finding causes of muscle weakness or paralysis; muscle problems such as muscle twitching; numbness, tingling or pain; and nerve damage or injury.

An EMG can be done in a doctor's office, hospital or lab by a nurse, doctor, or x-ray technician.

How is an EMG done?
The EMG takes thirty to sixty minutes, depending on the number of muscles to be tested. A small metal needle is inserted through the skin into the muscles to record impulses or electrical activity in the muscle. The doctor will read the EMG when your muscle is resting, when it is contracting slightly (for example, by bending your arm), and when it is contracting with more force.
The needle or electrode position may be changed and the process repeated four or more times in the same muscle for a more complete study. The results are studied to determine the cause of the muscle problem.

At the same time as the EMG, you may also have a nerve conduction velocity (NCV) test to rule out disorders of the nerve or nerve injuries that may be affecting the muscles. For this test, electrodes are placed on the skin to measure the activity of the nerves. Some people report feeling discomfort or pain, depending on the muscles being tested.

After the test, you may have mild aching for up to six hours, followed by soreness and tingling in the muscle that was tested for one or two days. You may also have a small bruise that lasts for a week or more.

Magnetic Resonance Imaging Scan (MRI)
 A magnetic resonance imaging scan, or MRI, is used to see small changes in the body that cannot be seen with a normal x-ray. Magnets and radio waves are used to make a computer picture of the parts of the body the doctor wants to study. If you have myositis, the doctor may study the affected muscles using an MRI to get a better picture of any muscle damage.

With an MRI, patients are not exposed to radiation like they are with the traditional x-ray. An MRI is also more accurate in finding what may be causing your pain or weakness.

There are no known side effects with an MRI, but some people should not have these scans. Pregnant women are advised not to have MRIs. If you have any foreign materials in your body, including artificial limbs or joints, tell your doctor. If you have a pacemaker, chemotherapy or insulin pumps, or any metal implants or chips, you cannot have an MRI because of the magnets used.

You will need to lie still in a closed tube for 30 to 90 minutes, depending on what parts of the body are being studied. You will hear a loud clicking noise during the test. You will be placed into the tunnel-like tube where the magnet and radio waves will work together to produce a detailed image for the doctor to study. If the doctor needs to see more detail, you may be given an IV with a special liquid to improve the images.

Definite diagnosis of inclusion-body myositis can be made if muscle biopsy features are diagnostic:
 Invasion of nonnecrotic fibers by mononuclear cells
 Vacuolated muscle fibers
 Either intracellular (within muscle fibers) amyloid deposits by fluorescent method of identification or 15-18 nm tubulofilaments by electron microscopy.

There...if you understood any of that you are more knowledgeable than most doctors are concerning this disease.

Chapter Twenty-one

Going Down

The most feared sound my wife hears is the sound of me falling on the hardwood floor in the kitchen. For some reason, the kitchen floor is the most popular place for me to fall. No, it's not because I spend a lot of time scoping out left-overs in the refrigerator. I think it has to do with how my tennis shoe can catch the surface of the floor when the front of my foot does not raise properly, something that's called "foot drop". When the front of the foot catches the floor surface before it should, it interrupts the normal foot and leg movement, tripping me and down I go. It often seems like it is occurring in slow motion, but one thing for sure is….that I'm going down and there isn't anything I can do to stop it, so I have to play defense and try to minimize injury while it is happening. It doesn't pay to try to catch myself with my arms as they do not have the strength required to do so. I try to fall forward if I can, because several falls where my knees just collapse underneath me, my fall often resulted in server foot pain then the foot and toes get bent in a direction that they are not supposed to bend.

People often ask me if I am getting better. No, you don't get better with IBM. It may seem like I am getting around better, but it's just learning to play with the cards I have been dealt that makes me appear I am doing better.

I believe there is a point in time with IBM where the falls decrease for a period of time. This phenomenon is not due to a stoppage of muscle loss, or a reversal of muscle loss. I think it is just a period in time where "we" have adapted to "how to walk" without falling, whether it is only the conscious effort to pay more attention to every step, or an actual modification in how we walk. Unfortunately, this works for a while until your muscles or lack of muscles decide they don't want to support you anymore and you will start falling more often again. I am in the transition between the concentrating on every step and falling more often. I fall when I forget to think about every step, or if I let my front foot drop and my shoe catches the floor before it's supposed to. I am spending more time in my powerchair and have less bumps and bruises because of using the powerchair, and feel more independent using it. But that is part of the prescription for not falling as often.

I use my Pride Quantum 6000Z powerchair to help me up into a standing position. This powerchair has a feature that allows the entire seat part of the unit to rotate backwards. As the leg support pads move with the seat, I am able to tip the seat backwards and the thigh pads on the footrest arms help push the back of my thighs forward until I am in a standing position. For now, this approach works excellent for me, but in the future, I may have to resort to purchasing a "standing" powerchair or one that the seat actually raises the user up to a near vertical position. These types of chairs are popular to combat these aspects of being wheelchair bound and provide:

1. Increased bone density
2. Decreased leg spasticity
3. Decreased pressure sores
4. Improved bowel function
5. Improved bladder function
6. Decreased respiratory and gastro-intestinal complications

Gee, I would hate to add any or all of these on top of my myositis.

Chapter Twenty-two

Show Me Your Guns

Any mass shootings in the USA are a terrible tragedy. In fact, any pointing a firearm at any individual is a tragedy. People who respect firearms know it is not right to point a firearm at anyone unless in self-defense. People who have a Conceal Carry Permit know how to respectfully handle a gun. Hunters respect their firearms and usually practice safe use of them.

Since 2001, more than 5000 people have been killed in Chicago with firearms. In that same timeframe, 2000 soldiers were killed in the war in Afghanistan, many of them from the effects of an explosive device and not by gunfire.[14] These killings were not caused by people with hunting rifles or sportsman's handguns.

In January, 2013, Chicago recorded 42 deaths by gunfire, the most for that month in their history.[15] Chicago has some of the strictest gun control laws in the country, but continues to have the highest murder rate with guns in the nation. Their largest problem is now to find the prison space to house all the convicted gun felons, because Chicago has run out of prison space.[16]

Felons who typically may receive seven years for their firearm crimes are released in two years because of overcrowding. With handguns as easy to get in the "hood", an early released criminal can secure the use of another firearm the same day he is released from the prison.

---

[14]   http://www.huffingtonpost.com/2012/06/16/chicago-homicide-rate-wor_n_1602692.html
[15]   http://www.chicagotribune.com/news/local/ct-met-chicago-murder-decade-20130215,0,2528357.story
[16]   http://www.chicagotribune.com/news/local/ct-met-chicago-murder-decade-20130215,0,2528357.story

So what are the firearm laws like in Chicago?[17] To get a Firearm Owners Identification Card, you must be a resident living in Illinois who:

•*Is over 21 years of age? If under 21, he must have the written consent of his parent or guardian. In such case, the guardian himself must not be ineligible for a Firearm Owner's Identification Card (FOID), and the applicant must never have been convicted of a misdemeanor or adjudged a delinquent.*

•*Has never been convicted of a felony.*

•*Is not a narcotics addict.*

•*Has not been a patient in a mental hospital in the preceding five years.*

•*Is not mentally retarded.*

•*Is not an alien, who is unlawfully present in the United States.*

•*Is not subject to an existing order of protection prohibiting the possession of a firearm.*

•*Has not been convicted within the past 5 years of battery, assault, aggravated assault, violation of an order of protection, or a substantially similar offense in another jurisdiction, in which a firearm was used or possessed.*

•*Has not been convicted of domestic battery or a substantially similar offense in another jurisdiction committed on or after January 1, 1998.*

---

[17] http://crime.about.com/od/gunlawsbystate/p/gunlaws_il.htm

•Has not been convicted within the past five years of domestic battery or a substantially similar offense in another jurisdiction committed before January 1, 1998.

An applicant for a FOID must consent to the Department using the applicant's digital driver's license or Illinois ID card photograph, if available, and signature on the FOID, and must furnish the Department with his driver's license or Illinois ID card number.

Where does the local Chicagoanite get a gun from when he needs one quick? You might think they are sourcing guns from neighboring states, but that answer is wrong by a long shot. Fifty-eight percent of the guns recovered after a crime was previously purchased right in Illinois, the State with the tough gun laws. Only nineteen percent came from next door, Indiana, and three percent from my home State of Wisconsin. [18] The other twenty percent were probably purchased locally from fellow gang members or other illegal source that is untraceable.

There are many guns that are purchased legally by citizens who do not have a felonious past and probably even possess a valid FOID. But they either resell them on the open market under the radar of the local law, or sell them and report them stolen. If a person wants a firearm bad enough, he will be able to readily find one. Felons being released early from the Illinois or Chicago prisons probably have an arrangement for buying a new "piece" before the ink is even dry on their release papers.

There is no problem facing America today that liberals do not believe cannot be solved by more government and less freedom, and Chicago has tried to prove that theory. The fact of the matter is that the total black population in the Chicago area own less firearms than the average U.S. citizen,

---

[18]   http://www.suntimes.com/news/crime/14715658-418/chicago-gangs-dont-have-to-go-far-to-buy-guns.html

therefore are considered to be less protected and defended. According to a recent Pew Research Center survey, forty-two percent of whites and only sixteen percent of blacks say that they have a pistol or rifle at home. Because of this, blacks are more likely to be the targets of gun toting gang members looking for an easy kill.

More gun regulations in the USA will probably not help the crime rate one bit. Chicago, that has the strictest gun control regulations in the USA also possess the crown for having the most murderous crimes in their community.

Just as no one mandates that anyone must own a gun, it should also be apparent that no law abiding citizen should be deprived of owning one either.

Chapter Twenty-three

Gullibilitation

There, I did it! I made up a new word. **Gullibilitation**.......*an act to persuade a large mass of naïve people to accept a creation of a phenomenon for political purposes.*

Sound reasonable? Okay, let's run with it. Hopefully your local bookstore is ordering new dictionaries that have added this word as we speak! Listen for this new word to be included in your son or daughter's next spelling bee.

The American population is so naïve, so gullible these days. Some people would believe that if the President said he wanted to take some weight out of the dumbbells at your local health gym so more people would use them there would be a number of people who would support that notion. When the President tells you things in the economy are looking up, that doesn't necessarily mean things are getting better. It's a fact that we are experiencing a recovery that is no better than the recession we were said to be in. The latest estimates from the Census Bureau show that the median income for U.S. households in 2011 was $50,054. In 2009, the year the "Great Recession" ended, the median income of U.S. households had been $52,195 (in 2011 dollars). Thus, in the two years since the so-called "end" of the recession, median household income has fallen by 4.1%.[19] How many times have you heard the President or the liberal news media say that?

Likewise there are a number of people in the USA who think that new trade agreements with other countries will add jobs and boost exports and cause the economy to soar. "And tonight, I am announcing that we will launch talks on a comprehensive Transatlantic Trade and Investment

---

[19] http://www.pewsocialtrends.org/2012/09/12/a-recovery-no-better-than-the-recession/

Partnership with the European Union -- because trade that is free and fair across the Atlantic supports millions of good-paying American jobs." [20]

Here's a little history about this subject: In 2012 exports to Europe fell. Imports from Europe rose an alarming 16% causing a trade deficit with them of $116 billion. How did the trade agreement that we signed with South Korea help us? Since that time, our trade deficit with South Korea has worsened by 25%. These alarming figures are not presented in the President's speech to solidify his proposed action for additional trade agreements with those countries, but because the President made that statement in the State of the Union Address, it must be so! You must not believe everything just because a politician spews it out of his mouth, but rather make your judgment on his successes and failures. In this case, it is evident that the South Koreans and European businesses and countries are "eating our lunch", and taking advantage of us. What about our trade with Japan? Last year (2012) our trade deficit with Japan was over $76 million. The word "deficit" means we are buying more from them than they are buying from us! Isn't this more evidence that either the people in power are totally absent when dealing in the business world, or is it a sign of them carrying out a very malicious plan to devour the United States of America from within?

And what about that Affordable Care Act, better known as Obamacare? Democratic Congressmen across the spectrum supported the controversial bill, without knowing what was in it. Now, two years after the bill was signed, and it is ready to be implemented fully, there are questions by everyone what the bill actually contains. It is also evident that there are a bunch of government Shetland ponies in Washington, DC that are trying to figure out how to implement many parts of Obamacare, and people in the Health and Human Services

---

[20] http://www.whitehouse.gov/state-of-the-union-2013

are making things up as they go. The costs are skyrocketing compared to what was promised during the run up to passing the bill. Obamacare will not be saving any citizen any money as currently stated, but rather will cost each family an average of $2500 more per year. And the American people were "gullibilized" again.

Anyone believing the global warming warnings should put down their protest signs and do a little investigation. How come it is only the friends and acquaintances of our Democratic Party members that seem to benefit the most financially from any anti-global warming initiatives? Is paying tens of billions for an unverifiable quarter degree in temperature difference really a good investment while turning a cheek to historical climate variations? How do you spell, "crony-selected beneficiaries?"

We often wonder how much of our charitable contributions actual go to the cause rather than into some administrator's pockets, and the same can be wondered here. The earthquake in Haiti is a good representation of this. Various groups tendered to the heartstrings of Americans asking for donations for the needy in that disaster torn country. But to date only about 35% of donations given to that cause have actually made a difference in that Caribbean island country. Now the subject has long been forgotten and people don't even think about where that money has gone. I think there is some more gullibilitation going on here.

Prior to the 2012 election, all the Democrats and their liberal news henchmen had to say was, "Romney is bad, Obama is good for America". This, said over and over without any other substantiating evidence, was enough to convince the naïve voters in most states. The Democrats pound into our heads over and over again that there is no voter fraud, and we must not mandate the voter ID laws in our states, but months after the election is over and nothing can be done to reverse it, there are countless cases of fraud in Ohio and Florida that have surfaced. Some voters in Ohio voted 6 times in an attempt to get Obama the win. It will be interesting to see if that gets any broadcast time on the left leaning newscasts. Want to bet?

As long as we are speaking of voter fraud, who's to say that some of the voting machines in busy districts weren't 'tampered with to give the slant to a certain party. This conspiracy possibility might pass the eyes of government election officials that don't know the inner workings of a computerized device. If people don't understand how a simple digital microwave can automatically adjust the time to daylight savings time or how a cell phone works, why would they not wonder if some electronics guru couldn't find an undetectable way for a voting machine to misrepresent the popular vote or the summation of the votes on Election Day? I'm just saying.....

And it doesn't matter how many times we are told by our leader that he has made the economy better, there is proof that the American black citizens have less jobs in 2012 than a year earlier, and less jobs than the year before and jobs for legal Hispanics are also down. Fewer women are working in jobs when compared to a year ago, but this matter doesn't get the media attention that it deserves, because telling the truth might just injure the credibility of the Democrat's sitting head of the White House.

Here is my plan. If I use the word "gullibilitation" enough times, people will eventually know what it means and will believe it as an accepted word. This also happens in the socialist takeover of America. If you can get the Democrats in Congress, the media press and others to talk about something often enough, the gullible people in the USA will believe it as fact and the it is a good thing, regardless of facts behind the story that are not being told. Example: Obamacare...people would listen to enough slanted press by the left leaning media, that soon people believed they couldn't live without it. On the other hand, if the left wants to spread a bad word around about the right, all they have to do is whistle and the media comes running to spread the dirt.

Rep. Pelosi stated, "we will have to pass Obamacare before we know what is in it"! If this isn't a sign of gullibilitation, then I don't know what is.

And what does Obamacare really mean to senior citizens? To have this discussion, you have to believe the fact that as a person ages, the necessity for healthcare also increases. The government realizes this also. You also have to realize that the "balloon" of baby-boomers will place a serious shortage of money in the piggy-bank when that age group starts hitting the rocking chairs. That time is now. You also have to wonder where all that money is going to come from as some of that Medicare (& Social Security) money disappeared years ago by appropriations by Congress to buy other things.

While the Affordable Care Act was touted as a huge benefit for people who do not already have medical insurance, it hurts the people who are already scrapping their pocket bottoms to pay for it now. Obamacare makes that pocket-scrapping a little tougher, because a lot of pockets have already been picked clean by tax increases, the slow economy and the higher cost of living, including gas, food, rent, insurance, clothing, and utilities, just mention a few.

As the baby boomers age, the probability of requiring additional health services also increase. Because there will be such a shortage of funds to take care of the aging baby boomers, we will likely see a gradual lessening of services allowed to this age group. Frankly speaking, the government needs you off the Medicare rolls because they can't afford you. The government wants you to die early to help them regain their solvency. Is it spelled out that way in the Obamacare document...of course not, but is it intended, I think so! Has the press accurately displayed this as a concern? No!

As long as we're talking about the press or media we should examine our own sources:

1. Do we always watch a particular newscast just because it comes on the channel right after a show that we regularly watch?
2. Do you live in an area where you only get coverage by particular networks?
3. Are you savvy enough to listen to different news channels, network and cable, to get a broad spectrum of viewpoints and then make up your own mind?
4. Does your favorite news channel only present one side of the story or does it adequately tell both sides of the story?
5. Do you ever go online to research any important issues, or do you just take what you hear on that one channel as being the "gospel truth"?

I feel that I get an almost equal valued distribution of media coverage. I have an email address account with AOL, which is associated with the Huffington Post, a left leaning organization. Whenever I pull up my account, the news for the day automatically appears on the screen, and anything of interest is usually read. I read our local newspaper, which is a left leaning publication owned by McClatchy. To get the other side of the story, I watch some Fox News on cable, that they do a fairly good job of interviewing both sides of each story. Late at night, I might watch some MSNBC, just to get a few laughs from their ultra-radical bunch of reporters before going to sleep. MSNBC deserves the low number of followers and poor rating that they have. Mr. Mathews and Mr. Ed couldn't speak the truth if their lives depended on it. They are laughable by what they say and also by what they refuse to cover, all in the name of supporting "their" chosen Commandant-in-chief!

It is no secret that the left receives millions of dollars from notorious outlaws like George Soros, who has a history of successes in orchestrating the collapse of various other countries. I had a discussion with a friend of mine that is from Malaysia, and now lives in Singapore, who didn't have one nice thing to say about the Soros "affect" on Malaysia during the 1990's.

George Soros has donated over $8 billion to assist and support the rebel rousing in the USA during the past couple of decades. The list of radical left-wing organizations that he has or is currently supporting is longer than my arm. In a CBS 60 Minutes program interview with Steve Kroft, Soros admitted his involvement with assisting the Nazi's raid on Jewish families, even though he was Jewish himself. One used to be able to watch several George Soros interviews on Youtube.com, but suspiciously the titles are still there, but the videos are no longer available. Hmmm. Is George Soros part of the Socialist master plan to upset the United States as he has contributed to almost all aspects supporting the Communist Party Goals of 1963? I would suspect he is.

Chapter Twenty-four

Our Money In and Out of Washington

In a time when our government officials should be caring for every penny they receive from taxpayers, they continue to amass larger and larger deficits year after year.

In the 2013 State of the Union Address, our President promised us a whole "new" set of priorities, that mostly resembled a lot of old priorities wrapped up in a new speech. And he claimed they wouldn't cost taxpayers a "single dime". I think we had this discussion previously in this book, but the reference to a "not a single dime" actually means he plans on covering these expenses with additional taxes on the American people, and lots of it. He didn't confer with other elected officials (Congress) about these expenditures, but blatantly carved out another path for spending money that he doesn't have yet.

He also announced the creation of a "Manufacturing Innovation Institute" starting in Ohio (probably in thanks to all his voters who carried him during the last election). What is this going to cost us, and where will the other 15 similar institutes be placed...in more blue states? How many of these institutes will become another Solyndra, feverously spending our money with little or no positive results? And will the money again go to businesses owned and run by the President's friends who will give back some of that money to fund the next socialist run up to the presidency?

The current administration has already run up additional debt to the tune of $5.9 trillion. This is more than the total of all his predecessors ranging back from Bill Clinton to George Washington. And he only shows signs of increasing that debt at a faster rate, and isn't worried since he doesn't have to coddle anyone for reelection. He will have all the money in his retirement and savings plans to be very comfortable in life, just like George Soros is, but doesn't care a bit about the average citizen who is being forced into a socialistic environment, whether they realize it now or not.

The odd way of accounting in Washington is probably the best example of gullibilitation found here in the USA. People are told almost daily how much money our government leaders are saving us every day. But the reality is that they count dollars for projects out in the future that "might" happen. Example: You go car shopping and look at a Chevrolet Malibu that costs $25,000 and a Ferrari California that costs you $192,000. You purchase the Malibu at $25,000 which is a difference of $167,000. If you tell your friends that you cut $167,000, they would look at you out the side of the eye sockets in disbelief of how stupid you must think they are. But if our President tells everyone that he cut $167,000 of spending by purchasing the car, many would tend to believe him and praise him for that move. He would also tell you that he is going to spend that $167,000 on an investment of the future, and some might tend to praise him some more. In reality, the president had to borrow the entire $192,000 from someone who needs to be repaid with interest. He never tells you the payment plan or how much interest it's going to cost you in the next twenty years. But he will tell you he saved $167,000 for you. In reality, he wasn't ever going to buy that $192,000 item, but conjured up that story to make him look like he's saving you money. Add about three or six zeros onto that example and you will appreciate the numbers he "plays" with every day. He'll attempt to impress you with those fake numbers to hide what he is really spending.

In the end, all the stories in the world won't hide the fact that he's borrowing forty-eight cents out of every dollar he spends, and the piper will need payment when he is no longer in office,...so he doesn't care.

The Quote of the Decade: "*The fact that we are here today to debate raising America's debt limit is a sign of leadership failure. It is a sign that the US Government cannot pay its own bills. It is a sign that we now depend on ongoing financial assistance from foreign countries to finance our Government's reckless fiscal policies. Increasing America's debt weakens us domestically and internationally. Leadership means that, "the buck stops here.' Instead, Washington is shifting the burden of bad choices today onto the backs of our children and grandchildren. America has a debt problem and a failure of leadership. Americans deserve better."*[21]

Too bad that same young inexperienced lawmaker doesn't believe the same today. Instead he is doing just the opposite.

Taxes

People who say that we don't pay enough taxes probably are either not paying attention or have no responsibility for money. Let's look at a list of some of the taxes we pay for:

Interesting List of Taxes that exist today:

Accounts Receivable Tax

Building Permit Tax

Capital Gains Tax

CDL license Tax

Cigarette Tax

Corporate Income Tax

Court Fines (indirect taxes)

Dog License Tax

Federal Income Tax

Federal Unemployment Tax (FUTA)

---

[21] Senator Barack H. Obama, March 2006

Fishing License Tax

Food License Tax

Fuel permit tax

Gasoline Tax (42 cents per gallon, varies by state)

Hunting License Tax

Inheritance Tax Interest expense (tax on the money)

Inventory tax IRS Interest Charges (tax on top of tax)

IRS Penalties (tax on top of tax)

Liquor Tax

Local Income Tax

Local surcharge taxes

Luxury Taxes

Marriage License Tax

Medicare Tax

Property Tax

Real Estate Tax

Septic Permit Tax

Service Charge Taxes

Social Security Tax

Road Usage Taxes (Truckers)

Sales Taxes

Recreational Vehicle Tax

Road Toll Booth Taxes

School Tax

State Income Tax

State Unemployment Tax (SUTA)

Telephone federal excise tax

Telephone federal universal service fee tax

Telephone federal, state and

Telephone minimum usage surcharge tax

Telephone recurring and non-recurring charges tax

Telephone state and local tax

Telephone usage charge tax

Toll Bridge Taxes

Toll Tunnel Taxes

Traffic Fines (indirect taxation)

Trailer Registration Tax

Utility Taxes

Vehicle License Registration Tax

Vehicle Sales Tax

Watercraft Registration Tax

Well Permit Tax

Workers Compensation Tax

"Not one of these taxes existed 100 years ago and our nation was the most prosperous in the world, had absolutely no national debt, had the largest middle class in the world and only one parent had to work to support the family."[22]

There are probably some additional taxes that you pay that are not on this list. A few that I can add to the list are:
Airport User Tax

Airline Fuel Surtax
Special Hotel Tax

We are not under-taxed, we are over-spending!

Chapter Twenty-five

Paralyzed

As President John Adams said, we have "a government of laws, and not of men."

The unnatural and unhealthy tendency to worship the people that temporarily fill government positions is a distraction for young people who should be focused on their own efforts to find their way in life.

Our country is headed to a point in time where it won't be able to do anything because of the vast amount of debt that it has generated. Normal citizens won't be able to function as we do today or did for the last two hundred years. Our freedoms will have been stripped away from us a little at a time. The Socialist way is to divide and conquer, and the transformed Democrats have been successful in making that come true. We are further apart from each other than we have ever been in the history of our country, mostly by design of the recent administrative directions. One party leans towards socialism, while the other party leans towards capitalism and Americanism.

Now we are faced with the likelihood of sequestration cuts that will weaken our military in a time that the Iranians and North Koreans are developing weapons of mass destruction and are promising to use them on us. And there are not enough people who remember World War II to remember what things were like back then or even in the early 1960's when everyone depended on air raid sirens to work properly.

Go back to the time of the USA entering World War II. America had the 16th largest military, right behind that of Spain. Our aircraft was no match to that of the Germans and the Japanese. It took some fast and furious actions to make our fighter planes equal to that of the Germans. At first we were losing that battle, but surged ahead of them later in the war to defeat them. Since our challenges are now in the nuclear age, is this really the time to be decreasing our stock piles of nuclear arms like the current administration is proposing? Is this just playing into the idea that we must become a weaker force in the world subject to takeover by our foes? Our foes are crazy enough, but smart enough to figure out a way to lob a missile with a nuclear warhead on it into a populated area of our country. Will it be on New York, Boston, Philadelphia, or Washington D.C.? Or perhaps they will sneak a sub off the shores of California and paralyze Los Angeles. How about them lofting the missile into Ohio and let the nuclear matter drift across the whole eastern region of the USA?

My future is a paralyzing thought also. My IBM has already taken away all my hobbies and activities, and at age 61 has made me surrender my auto driving to a more capable person. I have now fallen victim between my power chair, my lift recliner and my bed. America could be headed in the same direction in that they will not be able to do anything about their condition, and will be confronted with giving up all that the freedoms that we love. Again, I don't fear for myself. I fear for the future that is slowly creeping towards the destruction of our children and grandchildren's lives that is consuming us at a very slow, but steady rate. If everyone doesn't wake up pretty soon to what is really transpiring here in the good ole US of A, everyone will experience a loss in personal, economic and religious freedom.

Chapter Twenty-six

Plight of the Black

I have worked with, played with, traveled with, and ate with many blacks in my lifetime. I hope I never gave anyone a sense that I had a trace of racism in my body, I believe in the phrase, "All men are created equal" as much as anyone.

It didn't bother me when I heard people say that we finally elected a black person into the White House, even though I knew there were other mixed race Presidents already entrenched in our country's history books. But it does bother me somewhat when I hear anyone complain that our current President isn't doing enough for black people. I'm not sure what they expected, but I have a problem with anyone, white, black, red, yellow or brown, saying that they think a President with a certain skin color should take special care of their own race. Our founding fathers did not intend that to happen, and we shouldn't either.

On the other hand, President Obama is inviting divide between races when he addressed the Congressional Black Caucus and says, "Take off your bedroom slippers, put on your marching shoes.", as he said in 2011, inviting blacks to march with him to a better life. That better life isn't going to appear out of nowhere, and a recent USA Today/Gallup Poll indicates that 64% of black people polled saw no change or a turn for the worse since President Obama took office in 2008.[23] I can't imagine how President Obama's plea for blacks to hit the streets is in any way a constructive means to improve their lives. If anything, it may cause further racial divide with those who were neutral.

---

[23] http://caffertyfile.blogs.cnn.com/2011/09/27/has-president-obama-made-racism-worse/

A little history tells us the Democrats after the Civil War did everything they could to prevent the end to slavery, and out of this tension, the Ku Klux Klan was formed, of course, by Democrats. As the old saying goes, "It is one thing to see racism where none exists- and quite another to point it out where it actually does." I'm not sure what our President is going to do going forward, but so far his attempt to do anything for the blacks have seemed to be non-existent. But he's keeping his crowds happy by piling on the government freebies that some say will only hurt the racial problems further.

Chapter Twenty-Seven

Real MMA Fighting

Sort of a misleading title to this chapter, isn't it? I bet you thought I was going to talk about those brutes that entertain others by beating the crap out of their opponents in a cage for fun. Not so.

This short and sweet chapter can be summed up in a short verse written by Father Denis Edward O'Brien M.M. USMC:

> *It is the soldier, not the reporter, Who has given us freedom of the press.*
> *It is the soldier, not the poet, Who has given us freedom of speech.*
> *It is the soldier, not the organizer, Who has given us the freedom to demonstrate.*
> *It is the soldier, Who salutes the flag, Who serves beneath the flag,*
> *And whose coffin is draped by the flag, Who allows the protestor to burn the flag.*

It's sad to see our current government administration so blatantly attempt to weaken our military. It's seems okay to them to dole out a bunch of taxpayer dollars to fund a study of the sexual habits of Brazilian insects, but show a constant effort to defund our military. I can agree with the elimination of unnecessary waste in the military, but do not agree with actions that make our armed forces weaker and more susceptible to danger. As stated in a previous chapter, our armed forces were very weak entering into World War II, only necessitating us to accelerate our abilities while the war was causing us unnecessary casualties. We gained a superior warfare capability during the height of the war because the USA was a manufacturing giant in the world and could adapt to successful means of defeating the enemy. History tells us that many of our country's businesses were quickly transformed into war supply manufacturing plants. As we have now given up our manufacturing giant status to China and Mexico, how quickly would we be able to adapt to our nation's needs if another World War would break out? I seriously doubt if the Mexicans or the Chinese would build war good for us. How many men and women in the services would be sacrificed because of inability to quickly adapt to the needs of the war?

Everyone should learn that America is no longer the land of engineers. For decades, we could stand tall at the top of the engineering ladder. But in the last twenty years, while our college borne student was shrugging off the tough college majors for the lite and elite classes, our competitors in Asia and Middle East have been accelerating their training of qualified engineers.

Many will remember when there were only American raised doctors joining clinical practices here in the USA. Now, you are lucky to be referred to a specialist that is of American ancestry. Look in the phone book and see how many foreign doctors have now blessed our physician ranks. The same is true for engineering people, but not as easily recognizable by picking up a phone book.

If or when the world erupts into another serious war, will the USA be ready or will it take another 9/11 or worse to wake us up?

Last Chapter

Why did I mix my IBM & politics in this one book?

I actually wrote this chapter first. I admit it, I did it.

There are so many similarities between having a disease like Inclusion Body Myositis and what the USA is unintentionally or intensionally becoming, that I'm not sure there is enough paper to express them all. Both have been infested in ways that are ultimately undesirable, some noticeable, some not so noticeable.

If history is said to repeat itself, we are in the midst of doing exactly that. King George III, from his distant throne of England & Ireland, tried to influence the citizens of the new colonies, later to become the United States of America, and said, "The colonists must either submit or triumph," and extended Parliament's version of an "olive branch" in early 1775, when the English government offered to desist from taxing any colony that made adequate provisions to support its civil and military government. But then Parliament proceeded to pass laws restraining trade and fisheries in New England, and later in all the colonies. The "olive branch" offer did not succeed and the first shots of the war were fired a few months later.[24] The leader was instilling taxes and trying to limit people's rights, similar to what is beginning to brew again in the new millennium.

Like IBM, the disease that I didn't want or could even fathom, the thought of ever getting, the slow, onward march quietly progressed below my instinctive radar, until it manifested itself to a full time condition that one is forced to accept as the new norm.

---

[24] http://www.shmoop.com/american-revolution/king-george-iii.html

Although I was not diagnosed with IBM until 2007, I can look back and realize all the signs that indicated a changed direction. Each one by itself did not raise a serious concern, but the study of all the small indicators in total make for a disease that cannot be reversed. When I thought I just need more exercise to build up my leg muscles in 2004, I wasn't aware it was the result of a disease that would change my life forever. I tried to fight against the ill-perceived notion by steadily increasing my leg squat exercises on my son's work out machine. But if you can't predict a serious situation because of a historical past of good health, one doesn't expect that an outside force can overcome oneself.

There are some "haters" in the world that want the USA to go down! These haters are not only the recent offenders we see every day, but stretch back decades in time. Becoming aware of what led the Bill Ayers and Saul Alinsky's of the world to do what they do, and do what they did, should raise everyone's eyebrows in disbelief that we just sat back and watched it happen. It was slowly and silently taking over our well-being, and continues down that path today.

Because good planning was a major part of the Socialists or Communists years ago, we have now accepted certain changes as the "norm", and reversing it is unlikely. But that's the way the plan was laid out; not by taking large steps in forcefully take us over, but by taking very small, baby steps, sometimes undetectable, and irreversible.

I can read other IBM patients accounts of what their past involved and what they considered their new "norms". If we dissect some of our nations' past, we can also see the small indicators and the intended direction of our foes.

I know I will be bedridden in the future at some point, and also realize that that is clearly the direction that our foes want to take us in. It probably won't be in my lifetime, but I seriously worry for the well-being of my children and grandchildren. We see our personal rights being challenged more and more every day, and see our liberties being erased by regulations and laws that are designed to change the way our founding fathers meant us to be. Soon, we will be just like European countries, not like the "new world" that was found for its people at the time of the first American Revolution in the 1700's.

Because we have the ability to see where others who experienced the same conditions have ended up, we should be able to somewhat accurately predict where our country is headed, just as I am able to predict where my IBM condition will ultimately take me. IBM is not considered a deadly disease, but it will purposely affect the way I exist, and none of those are pleasant. But since a majority of people are too busy with so many other unimportant things, the direction of this country is going unnoticed. Someday, a huge club will hit everyone alongside the head, just like the diagnosis of IBM did to me, and people will start to look back at the signs and say, "oh yeah," I see it now. But that "now" will be too late.

I'm sorry that the Democrats were the party that the foes decided to overtake. It was probably the weakest party at the time the future plan was established, and was the time when their party seemed the most vulnerable. I used to vote for various Democrats, and still do if I don't think they are part of the efforts to radically change America. Although many think it is time to update some things in America, a radical overhaul is not required. If the young radical liberals think it is their obligation to transform America into something it doesn't need to be, I'm afraid they are wrong.

History proves that radical change and redistribution of wealth, as well as the depressing losses of individual freedoms that are being pushed at us these days will only result in becoming something that we don't want to become, and something that our fore fathers warned us about.

If you do a little research you can learn about who influenced our Founding Fathers. John Locke, Baron de Montesquieu and Thomas Paine were solid influences to the writers of our country's founding documents. Locke, in one of his writings states his theory of natural rights (life, liberty, and property of people) and people have the right to pursue what they want without interference. He felt the laws of the land should be based on these rights, and if they are not followed then the people had the right to rebel. I believe the rebellion is only about 4 years away.

Montesquieu believed the idea of the separation of power within government. He felt power should be divided into 3 parts and each should check on the others. This kept an individual or a group from having too much power.

Thomas Payne wrote a draft of the Constitution as it stands now, and wrote it in an easy to read format and sold about 500,000 copies of his forty-seven page booklet, prior to the time the Constitution was written. The easy-to-read format and language was so the average, middleclass citizen could understand it.

Today's congressional legislative documents are prepared in "legalese", so no one can understand them. In fact, most of the members in Congress do not read or understand all the corners built into some of the documents.

In my battle with IBM, I notice 99% of people have never heard of it, so they brush if off as either a misnomer, or realize that they will never be unfortunate enough to get the disease that I have. True, there are only a couple of thousand people in the USA that have IBM, but I never thought I would get it either. I guess that I'm lucky that IBM is an older person's disease, with most cases occurring at an average age 55. Oddly, I was 55 when I was diagnosed, and lived a great and happy life prior to that time.

The rarity of IBM does not attract the attention of too many doctors. I love to see the expression on various doctor's faces when I ask them if they are knowledgeable of this disease. Most will admit that either they have only heard about it or have never heard of it. In a way, I guess that's good, because if every doctor knew about it, that would mean that there would be millions of people who have it. That would not be good. I don't wish this disease on anyone.

When I attend one of the Myositis events, either the annual national conference or at the quarterly local support group meetings, I get recharged by seeing other people fighting and coping with the same dilemmas, and realize how strong we really are to combat them. We all realize that we are becoming weaker each and every day, but somehow get up each morning and fight on, sometimes making due with the tools we prepare for ourselves, that make our day just a little more capable.

Now, if we could only get more people to wake up to conditions that surround them. America is weakening day after day, month after month, and year after year. Anyone that hasn't smell the air recently better take some time to do just that, before that big red door slams everyone in the face, this time with no chance of recovery or cure.

Epilogue

I originally intended to write this book for my children and grandchildren, so they will know a little bit about where I came from and what I am noticing in these unsettled times. Every time I drilled down into my life and my IBM disease, I saw a correlation to what is happening in our country today.

Both I and America are suffering through a dilemma that is probably incurable at this point, but America could wake up and stop the degradation of their people's liberties, where I cannot do the same with my IBM.

If there was an action that I could have taken ten years or twenty years ago to guarantee that I wouldn't have this condition today, I would have taken it, if for no other reason than for that of my family members and future generations.

Having visited forty-nine countries on our globe, and working alongside people who live in those countries, I am certain that the United States is the only place I would ever want to raise a family. I can only hope and pray that America can retain the liberties envisioned by our country's founders, for the sake of my children and theirs.

I am on my last legs, and sadly, our country might be too...!

May
God
Bless
the
USA